THERE'S NOTHING WRONG WITH YOU

REMEMBER WHO YOU ARE

BEYOND MEASURE
BOOK ONE

SLOAN LAUINGER

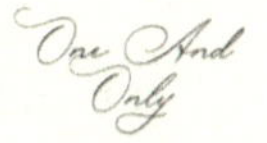

This book is a work of non-fiction. Any resemblance to actual persons, living or deceased, or actual events is coincidental, except where explicitly stated.

ISBN: 979-8-9933310-0-3

First Edition, Book One in the Beyond Measure Series

Printed in the United States of America

www.sloanmarielauinger.com

Published by One And Only

For the ones who choose truth over performance.
For the ones who refuse to settle for less than what's possible.
For the ones who won't sell out on themselves—or anyone else.

For those committed to evolving consciousness
in the name of harmony, expansion, creativity,
and love—over fear, stagnation, and war.

For every being and every event that has shaped me—
through love, kindness, honesty, shadow, and pain—
You make this what it is.

And to my late, great mother,
who was a voracious reader—
This one is for her, too.

What is essential is invisible to the eye.

— ANTOINE DE SAINT-EXUPÉRY

These passages arrived to me in a time of real need—and revealed a way of moving through life with much more calm, trust, and knowing than ever before.

You are always guided, protected, and provided for.

Psalm 23

The Lord is my shepherd;

He walks beside me and leads me to still waters.

He restores my soul; he leads me in the paths of righteousness.

Though I walk through the valley of the shadow of death, I will fear no evil. Thou art with me.

Use what God gave you to serve others—and do not dilute yourself.

1 Peter 4:10

As each one has received a gift, minister it to one another, as good stewards of the manifold grace of God.

CONTENTS

PART II: AWAKEN
PERCEPTION AND CHOICE

PART III: ATTUNE
FINE TUNE

PART IV: ASCEND
RIDE THE WAVES

RETURN

In the early morning of December 16, 1982, a little girl arrived.

Her parents had a hard time naming her.

In 2012, she woke up and recognized something she had always felt—

a disconnect.

No words to explain

but a truth felt.

The next day, she chose her name.

What follows is not linear.

It is a return—

to truth, to self, and to love beyond measure.

PREFACE

We build our worlds for safety long before we realize we're
doing it.
Look closely at the life you've architected—
the people, the patterns, the preferences, the relationships,
the pace, the tone. The calm, consistencies and clarity. Or
the chaos, confusion and unpredictability.
How you protect yourself is never without a trace.
I chased trends before I knew who I was.
The role I cast myself in was an outsourcing of my power.
It felt aligned—and safe. Until it wasn't.
Life can be played in many ways.
Choose the path that does not require you to turn a door
into a window. You do have choices.
This is a story about remembering—
that each of us holds power.
Do with it what you will.
And don't complain.

Architecture

Many of us sense something is off long before we can name it. A subtle distortion. A misalignment between who we are and how we're living. A fracture in who we are at the core. For me, it surfaces as frustration or depletion. A fine-tuning of the system—body, mind, soul instinct, and intuition—is what clears distraction, chaos, and confusion, and brings us back into harmony, ease, vitality, and alignment.

Throughout this book, we will acknowledge the body-mind and how, when it is attuned, *we are attuned*—and as a result—start remembering who we are and the power we hold. The power really is, quite literally, at our fingertips.

Despite what someone may have implied—there's nothing wrong with you—or me. It is about unlearning what was never yours. That which was cast upon you, or that which you adopted to be who you needed to be—moment to moment. It's time to release what's stuck, drop the over-calculation—a false sense of safety, and return to what is natural. Every breakdown is alive with information. Every asphyxiating moment and hesitation reveals something you can no longer ignore. Over-analysis and micromanagement will not get you closer. Honesty is what restores it.

Seasons

There were seasons when my nervous system could not handle more. I ate the same few foods on repeat because familiarity was less exhausting than choice. I tolerated things then that I would never tolerate now—people, situations, experiences. I was strategic with my energy bank because I had to be. There was only—so much.

There are forms of self-abandonment that can be tough to recognize. They look steadfast and loyal. Some even look like kindness or love. You suspend in high-function; you prolong the inevitable and put yourself last. You dim your light—not to be seen and heard, but to keep the peace and maintain tone for everyone else. It doesn't feel dramatic at the time. But it adds up. A slow erosion of the soul. This, today, right here—is where self-worth returns. When you stop unconsciously fitting in to be chosen or to protect yourself, and—you start choosing yourself. Shining brighter than you ever have before.

This book promises nothing except insight into thinking differently and offers companionship if you are going through it.

We all have our own version of 'it'. What is true will remain. What is false will fall away.

The topic of love is woven through these pages. Not strictly romance—but love as core stability. As a decision that translates into unshakeable inner authority. It does not shout or beg; it simply opens the door—to a different place.

What you refuse to face will run you. What you face will free you. Let's go.

INTRODUCTION

I was a contented child and not unhappy.
But I learned early that peace had a price tag.
I became good at reading rooms.
I understood the temperature before it surfaced.
Disappointment before it was spoken. A sharp glance.
I adjusted accordingly.
By the time I was four or five, I understood tone. And mistakes cost warmth and affection.
Early on, I understood how to strategically respond.
In the midst of my twenties, I had forgotten what my own sense of self sounded like—running off of programs and paradigms I wasn't conscious had been installed. In an attempt to simply find my way—I mistook character adaptation for identity, as many of us do. And so the beginning of the unravelling began.

While writing this book, early one morning while washing my hands, a sentence surfaced: Nothing erodes you like the quiet prison of living out of alignment. Living a life you wake up one day to realize is not yours. I learned that the hard way. More than once.

I grew up on manicured lawns and homemade meals. Rose bushes outside the house until we moved. My parents divorced when I was four or five. Sad in the moment. Not a tragedy. The show must go on. A small town with deep-freeze winters that stung your face on the walk to school—the kind of cold that has no words. You can live in one dream and long for another. For as small as my two-thousand-person hometown was, it was a real community. Sports, rink food (core nostalgia), cabarets, farmer's markets, rodeos, live theatre, trusted professionals, homeopathic medicine and acupuncture. Family-run restaurants, white picket fences with lilacs and hydrangeas, real neighbors. There was a lot to appreciate. And I did. While intently dreaming of a different life. Even then, I knew I wasn't built for that paradigm. I prayed for hot sun on my body. For beach mornings and ocean air on my skin. That dream came true.

My mother lived with a chronic illness and worked three jobs. My father loved me, but lived far away, tending to another life. People carry their own worlds. Everyone has a private gravity. You learn acceptance for what is—early. It shapes how you attach. How you wait. What you tolerate and what you accept as love—or scraps. I wish I'd known that sooner.

Then came the pot-smoking stepbrother who never seemed to get in trouble—and his father, an enigma at the time, a man I now recognize as pure gold. To this day, I've never heard him raise his voice. Zero aggression, just calm and cool. He built us a basketball court and a fire pit. He cared for my mother when she was sick. Seals and Crofts still remind me of him stepping out of the garage on a summer afternoon. The most easygoing temperament to which I was not attuned.

As a child, I was obsessed with why people did what they did. I was curious. I still am. Some people don't tell you who they are; you simply feel them. Safe people radiate calm. The rest, your nervous system reads long before your mind finds the words.

When there's a void, you try to fill it.

To be seen.

Loved.

Chosen.

So you begin building a life you think might finally earn it. Being good enough for someone, in some way. I spent years shapeshifting into versions of myself that looked like acceptance, success, and safety. Doing the 'right thing' or the thing that 'made sense' at the time. It could be disputed that my version of the right thing was perhaps not—because I've never really been conventional.

In my early twenties, I started recognizing myself in certain women on screen. This was the beginning of reality television. And later in the context of fictional television shows—ones that fascinated me, here into recognition. It wasn't the beautiful parts of these lives I related to—it was who they were to be accepted, and what it created. The women had a certain type of exterior and demeanor. The one who agreed to her circumstances and made it look elegant. Subtle chaos framed as depth. Fragility that held its own type of power. That dynamic was one I was already fluent in. Instead of observing, I absorbed and became. I agreed to a role before anyone had cast me in it. I chose the character who adapted herself to be accepted. And eventually, I couldn't tell the difference. This version wasn't all bad. She surfaced emotions that needed to be felt. She revealed patterns that had been quietly running my life—patterns that kept me small, unhealthy, and limited. Eventually, she was a shell of her former self. The torching of this version eventually came. The irony? The person I kept abandoning held the power the entire time.

From the outside, the cost of what I traded didn't look like much. It looked intentional; consciously and unconsciously agreed upon. And it held true until it wasn't. The view was lovely, but there came a time I could not sleep. Mild self-loathing disguised as opulence. Luxury as a temporary sedative. Creativity as a bandage. Normalcy masking a soul starving for truth.

I didn't transform by becoming someone new. I resuscitated myself by unlearning who I had to become to survive. The roles. The numbness. The distractions we mistake for identity. The small addictions that protect us from the one thing we don't want to face: ourselves at the core. No matter how beautiful things appeared—or how unbearable they became, the truth remained the same: Nothing external heals what you refuse to see, feel, and change.

You can collect every shiny thing on earth, explore every beautiful corner of it, and still ache for something untouched in your soul. When I want something now, it's from desire—not the need for belonging. There is a difference. Being liked is not the purpose. Living is. I'm interested in being me—fully. And being free. The cost of freedom comes with its own set of taxes. And no matter the cost, the return is better than anything else.

My biggest turning points were not glamorous. They arrived quietly, decisively, without negotiation. Clear unwavering decisions. What felt like collapse was recalibration, a forced rebirth by God's command.

Rock bottom is sobering. Those who know—know.

It's when you decide you're done lying to yourself.

Done avoiding the inevitable.

It's when the body speaks—through exhaustion, dissociation, and a reflection you do not recognize.

Some memories are sharp, others foggy but heavy. Some remain buried, waiting for the moment they need to surface and be reconciled. Through all of it, one desire never moved: to be free.

This book is what it took to change the code to what nearly cost me my life. It didn't lead me to perfect. It led me to real, grounded, true and free.

PART I: IMPRINTS

ILLUSION OF IDENTITY

1

CHAPTER ONE

FORMING THE SELF

Imprints

BEFORE WE EVER LEARN TO CHOOSE WHO we are, we are shaped by the ecosystem we're born into. The tone of a home and the people within it. The unspoken rules and the emotional weather.

These early conditions write our first template—the story of who we believe we are long before we ever question it. In those early years, we're still trying to understand what life is. Some imprints become our most magnificent sparkle. Some become our darkest shadows. Both are part of being human, and both are required. There is no right or wrong in this department.

It took me a long time to realize there was nothing to fix—nothing inherently wrong with me. That understanding came only recently—at age 42, after years of trying to silence or outrun parts of myself that were never the problem. Those parts weren't flaws. They were information—signs pointing toward what I still needed to acknowledge.

If you've ever felt like a butterfly inside a glass jar, you'll understand. Enough air to breathe through tiny holes, but not enough room to live—or to fly an expansive life. That was childhood for me. Nothing out of the ordinary. I was cared for.

It all just felt contained—and deeply perplexing when I tried to imagine how I'd find my way to what I knew I wanted. There was an outsized gap to close. I could see the world outside the jar. And somehow, even then, I knew I belonged out there. In dreams, there was a way through. I saw and felt myself there. Even as a child, dreams were a refuge.

Memories That Ricochet

I remember the wind howling outside my frosty basement window, crawling into mismatched bedding. Some nights, the hot water was gone before I even got into the shower. Not devastating, it was just how it was. I was not ungrateful; I just knew there had to be more.

As children, we don't necessarily analyze these moments—but we do absorb them. The body remembers touch, tone, temperature, the energy of absence, and the feeling of comfort long before the mind assigns meaning. It stores experiences before the language of recognition arrives—and sometimes those experiences get buried, only to surface much later in life.

Years later, when I moved into my Miami Beach home from the Caribbean, I made a list of what I required. Everything was required. There was nothing in storage. Not a fork. Not a hanger. Nothing followed me except a few suitcases. The evening of arrival, my dogs and I ran out and got an inflatable mattress and the essentials. Ground zero, and grateful.

Later, when it came to making the list of needs, blankets were at the top of the list. Specific blankets. The weight, the texture. It wasn't about the textile—although it is always about the textile. It was about warmth at the end of the day—something dependable, something guaranteed.

As adults, we often give ourselves what we once went without. And I'm not talking about material things—while those too are valid.

Rewriting the Past

I rewrite my childhood in a softer light because I no longer need to remember how sharp things felt in order to see the truth of them. There is a difference between rewriting and denial. Rewriting is a conscious reshaping of what the heart continues to carry—an imprint you can finally exhale inside of. And yes, rewriting the past changes the present—and the future. Clinging to and rehearsing pain does not make you honorable. It makes you exhausted. When I learned I could change how something felt—without editing the facts—everything began to shift. Not overnight, but slowly. Like a gentle reveal.

Life repeats what the body cannot yet hold—lessons, tests, sensations asking to be felt, repaired, or released. Some absolutely incredible experiences slip through our fingers not because we didn't deserve them, but because we weren't yet equipped as the version of ourselves who could carry them.

The Emotional Weather of Childhood

I grew up around worry-energy—the quiet kind that settles into a room and disguises itself as being realistic or responsible: the destabilizing energy of anxiety.

Some people mistake worry for care. It isn't. Worry is fear in motion. I absorbed it without knowing I had a choice.

Anxiety truly is imagination betting against the self. There is a difference between preparedness and worry. Preparedness is calm, clear, and steady. Worry is exhausting. Perpetual. I used to run mental simulations constantly. What if this? What if that? If I could predict the outcome, I thought I'd be prepared. This false sense of control was not relaxing. It kept me tense. It did nothing productive. Yet it was baked into me. And mine to recognize and shake.

The Past as a Mirror

Every fear has a root. Every reaction has a beginning. The past defines you until you learn to look at it clearly—until you can meet it with compassion instead of judgment.

My childhood was full of micro-moments that compounded. A sigh of disapproval. A silence that felt like aloneness. A look that translated to you're disappointing.

My upbringing was humble and imperfect. More than enough. My family is genuinely good people. We were lower-middle class. I didn't know it. In the early 80s, I thought $30,000 a year and healthcare meant wealth. Perspective—changes. Life still felt abundant in many ways—and it was. My mother often left a plate by my bedside after dance class—cheese, apples, pickles, grapes, some kind of charcuterie meat. Care and love lived in the details.

She taught me that people are usually doing the best they can with what they have—that what you see isn't always the whole story.

I believed her then.

I still do.

2

CHAPTER TWO

INDELIBLE MARKS

Subtle Moments That Shape Us

We don't actually store memories—we store the meanings and feelings we allocate to them. Change the meaning, and the memory loses its grip and weight.

Life doesn't always teach through grand milestones or dramatic chapters. Most of what shapes us hides in the subtle, unremarkable moments: the angle of the morning sunlight, the way a room feels, a tone someone used once, a gesture of care that was small to them—but meant everything to you.

The stories that follow are not placed chronologically. They are tiny windows into the ordinary, where meaning hides in plain sight—as many wonders, secrets, and answers about the world do. God speaks through details and through people. What connects them isn't time, but consciousness. What looks small when you're living it often turns out to be sacred when you revisit it. It took me time to realize I often get what I expect to see.

A Lesson on Time

I was the kind of kid who respected time as if it were a living thing. Time value mattered to me. I deeply respected the time others shared with me—and I valued my own time.

My piano teacher, one of the kindest humans I've ever known—was often late or didn't show up at all. Not intentionally. Just life. Snowstorms, distance, domino effect delays. She had the best heart; she was just often—late.

I wasn't upset about missing lessons. I was irritated at what it implied: that my time didn't matter. Call me crazy at six or seven—it was what it was.

What I took away from many of my early days' commitments: show up in excellence. Be prepared. Respect the moment and everyone inside the bubble of it.

I was six, maybe seven, with compassion, but an intolerance for the disrespect of time.

A Lesson on Presence

There was a family I adored that wasn't mine. Not perfect. Not over the top. Just warm, consistent, and real. A bonus to get to be part of and witness for a short time.

I met them when I billeted at their home one summer during a dance intensive in the late 90s. The daughters, Nicky and Renee, were two different beings with similar DNA. Nicky was an exclamation mark of a human—direct, honest, vibrant, magnetic. Renee was poised and quiet in a way that spoke volumes—ethereal, soft-spoken, grounded, humble, the kind of presence that whispers louder than anyone trying to be seen. She just was.

Their parents moved through life side by side as loving

and respectful equals. Dr. Pugh had the kind of energy that made your whole nervous system exhale. Their mother, Christine—warmth was her leadership style.

Mornings in their home were not chaotic; they had a rhythm. Dance bags, hairbrushes, keys, backpacks. Everyone moving independently, yet somehow in sync. A house that quite literally danced to a shared heartbeat. There was always an extra seat at their table; always room for one more. Included automatically.

I'm sure they noticed my timid nature at the time, but they didn't try to fix it. They filled the gaps quietly, as if by instinct. With sincere compliments.

Their values were simple: health, expression, showing up, integrity, and commitment to each other. Everyone had their own world, and no one was left outside the others'.

Breakfast was ritualistic. I remember Dr. Pugh slicing a banana over each cereal bowl—methodically, intentionally, no rush. Soft-spoken. Each of us acknowledged. Everyone had places to be, but time slowed in that warmly sunlit kitchen. For the first time in my life, I felt something I didn't yet have words for: a foreign kind of relaxation came over my body. Safety. No tension. No rushing away to some place that felt more inclusive or comfortable. I belonged. Not conditionally. No need for modified behavior. Just the safety of being seen without earning it. Time—freely given.

The core four. They'll never know the imprint they left on me—how they showed me what care looks like when it isn't dramatic or transactional but is sincere, automatic and consistent.

My own home had love too, but it spoke a different dialect—one I wouldn't fully understand until much later. You don't realize how tightly you've been holding your breath until you understand what calm feels like. They showed me what was possible—and that is something important to hang on to.

Learn What's Really Being Said

My mother was effortlessly beautiful—green eyes, auburn waves, a tiny nose, perfect skin. People adored her: stylish, intelligent, funny, quietly magnetic.

She loved me, but affection was not part of her natural way of being. Her love didn't sound like "I'm proud of you" or "You're doing so well." It looked like motion: multiple jobs, long hours, no complaining, doing whatever it took so I could eat, dance, dream, exist.

As a child, I wanted comfort, time, and attention. What I received was steadiness. My wish was for hockey season to end so that her spare moments wouldn't be spent watching television. I now understand those 'TV moments' were far and few between in the grand context of things—necessary mental decompression, enjoyment, and relaxation. I just longed for—the attention of my mother.

Her commitment to providing was evident, but children don't read exhaustion from providing as love. We read it as though we were the burden. That we have caused a heavy weight.

So I learned early: don't burden people. Handle it yourself. Be easy to love. Ask for nothing. And maybe you will be loved back.

My mother had her own wounds—her silences louder than any lecture. She parented with reliability over vulnerability. It took years to understand what she was actually saying: she didn't love with her words. She loved with her actions. From her I inherited both strength and silence: self-reliance as default, self-abandonment disguised as independence, competence mistaken for personality.

For a long time, I wished she had loved me differently. Now I know she loved me the way she knew how—and in the exact way my soul needed in order to grow. That realization doesn't wipe away the ache of waiting for closeness or warmth. But it does make us human.

Wounds are only half the story. The other half is imprint—the traits absorbed unconsciously, codes written into the body that we came here with, the way someone's love becomes your blueprint for moving through the world. Endurance in any relationship is admirable. Without connection, it becomes starvation of the soul.

Some of my clearest memories of my mother come from the brief season when it was just us—after her divorce, before her longest-lasting love and life partnership began. I remember her buying patterns and materials and making my clothes. And my doll's clothes. Choosing and making what I ate with care. Creating beauty through intention. Blasting music and cleaning the house together. Pledging the furniture. I can smell the lemon on the hardwood living room furniture and the piano.

She was strict but soft. Effortlessly cool without trying. Impeccable taste in music. Loving without being emotionally available. A safe presence—when present. That gap shaped my attachment. One I've since healed and stabilized.

The Chateau

Some moments aren't lessons—and endings are beginnings. Some turning points you don't recognize until much later. Spring 2011. The garden at the Chateau Marmont was one of mine.

We weren't dating yet. We were sharing time, having fun and talking in the sun when something shifted. He asked a question I never expected: Would you share a life with me? Feelings and instincts have their own language. I would eventually discover there was a considerable age-gap between us; I thought he was 10 years younger. By the time I connected the dots I was beyond that detail mattering and prior to that it didn't register. This dynamic of relationship was never on my radar. People are people, and a meeting of consciousness was my thought at that time. In that moment, my heart knew the answer logic could have questioned.

It became a real relationship. Real skin in the game, real consequences. Grown children on the perimeter. A life fuller than mine at the time. It lasted its seasons. We tested and hurt each other. There came a point where our behavior and vision no longer matched, and our evolution drifted.

People romanticize karmic relationships because they don't know how frustrating they can be. They are not glamorous. They are work. They bring every unhealed part of you to the surface. They also give clarity you could not have earned any other way. Sometimes, the only way through is by experiencing.

Sometimes a relationship lasts because one person keeps believing while the other is already drifting. Not falling out of love at the same time. Conviction can keep two people afloat—until it disappears or changes direction. The ending wasn't dramatic. It was the quiet recognition that the season had shifted. Not because there was no love, but because the version of us in that garden was not who we were anymore. We both grew.

You don't need to defend a love that changed you. Not all love stories are meant to be permanent. Some love is meant to be profound and to expand you—into more of who you already are.

French Riviera Portal

Summer 2024. Some people are portals. Some arrive without warning and hand you keys—without realizing they've just opened a new timeline.

The day I met her, I had just arrived at the Grimaud countryside home that would be mine for the summer. The door opened, sunlight washing across the stone floor.

Salomé, the villa concierge, polite and composed. And then Kika, the property owner—the frequency woven through that home. Grounded. Elegant. Brazilian accent in a low, velvety voice. She wasn't there to impress—she simply was: clear, steady, no non-sense.

Recognition was instant. Curious. Unmistakable. We were both wearing a perfect white T-shirt—same fabric, same cut. Not matching, but mirror images.

My dogs wandered in like they owned the place. Kika scooped them up as if they were already hers. They melted into her. I exhaled for the first time in months. Soul recognition arrives fully formed and gives breathing room.

She showed me the space—crystal glasses, linens, tropical plants exactly where light knew them. We paused at an antique table. We didn't need to speak about it—we just felt the same thing. The renters who would move in after me replaced it with something replicated. One glance between Kika and me said everything: we saw beauty the same way. We appreciated the original.

Kika listened with her whole being. Hugged like she meant it. Spoke truth without needing agreement. She mirrored back a steadiness I had misplaced—my own.

The Darkest Day

June 2019. Palisades Bowl, Los Angeles. A Sunday that felt like a decade. Early head injury days felt mechanically repetitive. I wasn't going to bed early because I was tired. I was going to bed because sleep was the only break from the loop I was living.

Eighteen months earlier: a car accident. Phantom pain. Post traumatic stress. Post-concussion symptoms that lasted years. Income gone. Memory fractured. Executive functioning, unable to retrieve. Safety inside my own body—gone. Dissociation became normal. Like watching a version of me from the outside looking in. A soul, disoriented.

That's when the avatar was born—not a costume, but a lifeline. Something I could step into until my soul caught up.

I filmed a video that day: If you're going through it, I see you. Some days, there is just no light.

I never wanted to end my life. I love life. I want the most days on the clock with the people I love. At that time though, I wanted to end the version I was trapped in. There's a difference.

The thought passed. It never returned. Not because everything healed—but because something fierce resurfaced: I am not someone who quits. I play to win.

Healing was not a glow-up. It was repetition and

simplicity in solitude. One thing I have always been good at is discipline, especially when the going gets tough—and when something's at stake, like a life. Mine.

For almost a decade, it felt like an open-air prison. One stewarded by God, and architected by me. The less I resisted and the more I met my life honestly, the faster grace and clarity returned—alike laying brick into a solid foundation.

Keep going.

The Day the Grid Shifted

When your frequency changes, reality rearranges. Quantum leaps are real.

August 2023. A half-day layover in Miami. Three months before moving to St. Barths. Technically I'd been to Miami before—airport only. This time, my feet met the ground. I walked the beach—thick heat, salty air, wind so strong it felt like it could lift me. Every part of me decompressed. Then it happened. Not a metaphor. Not imagination. A blurring in front of me—like reality glitching. The grid shifted. The ground felt different. It wasn't excitement. It wasn't fear, it was stabilization. A knowing. As if I'd arrived somewhere that was long since programmed into me. Nothing changed externally, but something on the inside flipped forward that could not be undone.

Be Careful What You Wish For

I cannot even count how many times I have loosely said something—but fully meant it, and those very thoughts, once spoken, came to be. Fast.

I used to wish people and situations out of my life without understanding what I was doing. Not boundaries. Not decisions. Wishes—cast out of impatience. The wishes came to pass. And the magnitude in ripple was far bigger than I imagined.

One day around 2017, I prayed innocently: God, I wish I had an experience I could be a champion of—something I could use to help others. I didn't know that some prayers do not arrive as gentle, joyous miracles. They can also arrive as grueling initiations and gateways. In that prayer, the Universe did not hand me champagne, strawberries, and clarity—but instead, a fire to walk through.

3
CHAPTER THREE
UNTIMELY DEATH

Each soul arrives with an agreed-upon timeline—a window, a mission, an assignment with layers and corrections to master, integrate and evolve through. That timeline can shift through free will, choice, and circumstance. But eventually, there comes a moment when the soul departs its earthly assignment. Some stretch their time as far as they can. Some complete early—consciously or not. Others live without ever questioning the timeline or mission at all.

What matters isn't certainty or awareness of this. It's acceptance that no matter what, it is finite. And with acceptance comes power—so make it count.

What Loss Does

Loss is devastating—whether it arrives as an inevitable knowing, with time to brace and grieve in advance, or as a sudden shock with no warning at all. It can be debilitating.

Dissociative. It takes your breath away. We are rarely ready for it. Yet, somehow, we adapt. The show must go on.

I have witnessed grief move people in two very different directions. Some allow it to hollow them out—spiraling into decay, a ripple of compounding loss disguised as devotion to the one they lost. Those gone before us want us to live and rejoice, not suffer in penance. Others let grief refine them—deepening their capacity to love, to live and be open, to honor what mattered and be even more vibrant, expansive, and generous.

This chapter is not an instruction to bypass pain. It is an invitation to choose life with grief—not a life abandoned to it.

How Life Goes On

You will learn a new way to live, because the only way forward is through.

There is no playbook for loss. When physicality dissolves into memory, we must learn a new language of connection. I remind myself often: there are people who would give anything for one more day on earth. Do the thing—whatever it is, in honor of them. The workout. The trip. Diving two feet into love—or a project that scares the shit out of you. The conversation—forgiveness or making time for someone who matters. Even the small errands that once felt ordinary. Fresh flowers. My mother always had her nails done.

Every soul we tether to has a purpose. Grief asks us to recognize that purpose—and how it continues. Death becomes an uncompromising teacher of forward motion.

I've watched people freeze themselves in time, living inside memories that calcify into a catastrophic ripple of suffering. This happens in relationships too—holding on long after the lesson is complete. A clean cut, though painful, is healthier than a slow bleed.

Gucci Mules

Not long ago, I opened my closet and saw them: a pair of vintage chocolate-maroon Gucci platform mules. They were mine—yet instantly, I was transported back to the day I cleared out my mother's belongings. Her fragrance still clung faintly to the fabric, as if holding on for one last breath to be taken. Her presence lived in every space she had occupied—every textile, drawer, every earring.

Like wearing your spouse's shirt when your spouse is away—that temporary closeness, that fond fragrance baked into the fabric—was what I was harnessing in the moment. Only this time, there was no return.

I knew the moment was temporary. Eventually, the scent would fade. Her lived essence in those clothes would evaporate. The garments would release the language of her soul with no life being breathed back into them. The feeling of that moment became etched in my being.

Clothing is one of the most intimate echoes we leave behind. It touches our skin. It images our silhouette. It carries our stories without speaking. Closets teach impermanence very honestly. We are animated. When we go, what remains isn't the object—it's the feeling.

Creating Peace After the Fact

For years, I believed unfinished business was permanent—that closure required another person, another conversation, another moment. It doesn't. The final pages can be written alone. Forgiveness does not require another party or permission. This applies to any relationship—death or otherwise.

After my mother passed, the hardest part wasn't the absence. It was the ghost of what I wished I'd said more often. I hope she knew how much I loved her. I wish I could still make her proud. Grace is love that continues watching even after the room is empty.

Whether present or gone—if you've lost someone and still feel unsettled, let this be the moment you release them, not to excuse, but to free yourself. Holding resentment tethers you to pain. Forgiveness releases it and creates space.

The Call from Italy

Sorrento. June 2015.

I was thirty-two. My mother, fifty-five.

After thirty-six hours of travel, I turned on my phone. Messages flooded in. One from my aunt:

Your mom is in intensive care. It's serious. There's nothing you can do. Stay where you are.

Imagine arriving in Italy knowing your mother will not leave the hospital alive—and waiting for her to die so you can book a flight home to manage the aftermath. I would not have made it in time for her last breath. She didn't want me there to see her pass. She was strategic like that until the end. What shattered me came next.

My mother had lost her ability to speak—yet she kept trying to write. Her handwriting shaken. Her determination was intact—as always. She didn't want to go. She loved life—and she lived as such. Generous. Joyful.

Beautiful in every way. She didn't talk about it, she was about it.

She had lived half her life with a kidney condition. A transplant and care in nutrition and lifestyle bought her time. Then dialysis again. A routine hospital visit became an infection, which became sepsis. Her body couldn't fight.

I was enraged at a system where neglect was present. She blamed no one. She was grateful for the care she received.

The last memory I have of her is quaintly picturesque.

I opened the front door into the living room, about 3 months prior to her passing, a sight I had never imagined. She sat on the sofa, a walker beside her, decorated with balloons by Garry, her devoted husband. He always did things with such care. She stood slowly. Her voice was quieter. She was tired. Yet she went to the kitchen to make us lunch. Lemon chicken orzo soup her friend had dropped off. We shared it. A hug in her kitchen. I didn't know it was goodbye—and somehow, I did. I stared at her and knew this was it—just not when. We can know these things and still live in denial.

That embrace still lives in my body. I remember the feeling of her delicate bones through her cool skin. She didn't want to leave, but she had to.

Her passing reminded me of this:

Show up and live like it matters.

Regret Into Right

One regret I carry is that I saw my mother for who she really was—too late.

When it finally clicked, it felt as though another parallel came online within me, revealing how wrongly I had held her for most of my life. How could I, I remember thinking? For years, I mistook my own longing for a different life as something she had cemented me into—as though where I was, or what I hadn't yet claimed, was somehow her fault. Not resentment, exactly—but a quiet disdain I couldn't fully name.

Yet in real time, as far back as I can remember, I deeply appreciated everything she did. It was always more than enough. I often wished she'd had more support than she did. I never heard her complain once in the entire time she was alive.

What was missing was a me-thing—something intangible and unintegrated. I couldn't yet put my finger on it because I didn't yet know who I was, or where I was going. I knew what I wanted, but at the time it felt out of reach—and showed up as a flailing lack of ownership over my own life. You know—a bit of a self-loathing spiral. I know many can relate.

In mid-March 2010, we traveled to Boston together—the only trip we ever took. She was fifty. I was twenty-eight. It was unusually warm, one of those rare weeks where winter suspends itself and the city blooms into a temporary spring.

We walked through Boston Common alongside everyone else enchanted by the sunshine. We stayed at the Back Bay Hotel—best hotel robes, I might add. I remember watching her get ready in the morning, amazed by how little effort she required. Moisturizer. Glasses. Her natural palette was perfect. That was it. One cup of coffee. Angelic, really. Her aura often left me speechless.

I remember telling her how lucky her husband was to get to spend every day with her. And I meant it—fully.

I think we both saw each other differently on that trip.

Removed from daily life, given space to breathe. She saw her child—the one with a good heart, not the disappointing party girl she saw in everyday life. I saw her clearly, without projection or expectation.

In those moments, all either of us wanted was for the other to be happy. We each carried an unspoken mission to honor the other's choices. What we were doing did not matter. What mattered was that we were together—selflessly. Just that. A quiet magic revealed itself: unconditional love and acceptance.

The trip passed in the blink of an eye. And with it, something irreversible settled in me—the understanding of time's value, and of what actually matters.

Grief's Language

Grief softens what once protected you. It stretches the heart into new dimensions of compassion—and space.

Unmet, it calcifies. Met with grace, it transforms.

You only grieve deeply what you loved deeply.

Sometimes it feels like being underwater—holding your breath, waiting for a big wave to pass.

This wave doesn't really pass.

You learn how to breathe, ride the wave, move—and love, differently.

That's it.

Like Waves, They Hit You

Sometimes grief arrives before death. Sometimes long after.

If you've loved someone with memory loss, you know this terrain—missing them while they're still here.

That was true for me with my grandmother. When she passed—at ninety-four and a half—it felt like relief. For her, not for me. I wished she would have lived forever. She was ready, though. She had already lost her husband and two of her three children before her.

In a lucid dream, she, my mother, and my aunt were together. I wanted her to sit with us—but she was content in her chair.

That was when the real wave hit me. Three years later. The deepest cry. She was my protector. My best friend growing up for as long as I could remember.

While I speak of one grandparent here, each of mine imprinted me—as teachers, protectors, and guides. I loved each of them differently, and equally.

Love doesn't disappear. It just changes form.

They Reappear

In dreams, in nature—through others. Those who have left us are always reappearing. The day I said complete on this manuscript, we were walking. A peaceful, sunny Sunday. Sadie—one of my furry angels—turned us down an alleyway she never takes. When we came back out onto the main road, the front of the home we passed was covered in orange hibiscus. My mother's Instagram profile image: One large, beautiful orange hibiscus.

That was her saying, "get on with it". A very Deb thing to say. Who knew that small detour would bring that great reveal.

Magic and beauty are available for those who choose to believe and receive—and expect it. Always.

4
CHAPTER FOUR
LOVE

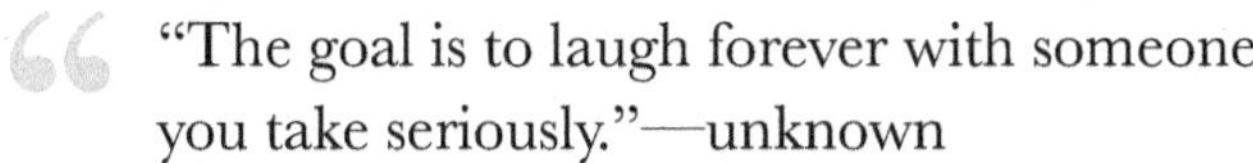

“The goal is to laugh forever with someone you take seriously.”—unknown

Relationships are a rigorous school. Few things evolve us faster. They reveal us. They refine us. That’s what they’re meant to do.

Love is foundational. And real love walks hand in hand with respect.

Even the most guarded heart will recognize itself here.

Love rarely arrives loudly. It shows up in ordinary moments—quiet, honest, unforced. It requires vulnerability, generosity, and truth.

Romantic love simply reveals us most clearly.

Once you’ve experienced a great love, anything less becomes obvious.

The Intertwining of Souls

Each person we become intimate with arrives for a reason. Every connection reveals something and leaves an imprint. Awareness is meant to inform progression—not delay it. This chapter isn't only about romantic love, but the lessons revealed through it. When you recognize that nothing is random—not the people who enter your life, not the patterns that repeat—confusion becomes informative. Pain gains context. Love becomes a teacher. People assign names to connection—soulmate, karmic, twin flame. Labels are optional. What matters is recognition. And recognition can happen more than once.

You remain the constant.

Given

I've never taken love for granted. In my life, it's always been present—family, friendships, romantic partnerships.

Both sides of my family poured it on, in their own ways. My mother's side gave time, presence, and provision. My father's side was generous too—and my grandmother smothered me with hugs, kisses, and "I love you's." Not occasionally, but constantly. Morning, noon, and night. Before entering the house and before leaving. I knew what love felt like early. Care. Inclusion. Being seen.

With a mother who worked and gave what she could, and a father who lived eight hours away, I learned to appreciate what was available. Any time was time I valued.

I don't remember always getting a call on my birthday. But I do remember a bottle of perfume. I cherished it—not for what it was, but for who it came from. I can still remember how it felt to hold on to something that meant I was thought of. I remember a beautiful dinner at upscale restaurant sitting together in the lounge, when I was seven or eight. My father said, "This is how a man should treat you." That memory etched. Presence came in moments, and I learned to hold on to them—sometimes longer than they lasted.

Stability and security felt fleeting—something that appeared, then disappeared. Cancellations were something I absorbed. I didn't have words to express the feeling back then. It's just something I got used to. Feelings that hinged upon the volatility of the external. Everyone in our lives is precious—but not guaranteed. We have ourself.
Everything else is icing—and I love icing. But settling for what's given has never been my way.

Maybe this is where the intentional carving of my own path began.

Invisible

My sense of self-worth in love was always strong—until it wasn't. That foundation began early. My dance teacher instilled it in me. She was protective over all of us. She didn't tolerate wasted time or misplaced attention—only people who were respectful, focused, and worthy of being in the room. The discipline and standards she set extended far beyond dance.

Self-worth is steady—until it's punctured. And when it is, it takes a moment to return to yourself. Yes, that moment could span more than a decade to recapture. To remember who you are—and move like it again, is the important part.

I was never physically harmed. But emotional absence leaves a its own hand marks. The wound of being invisible.

Of being excluded. Of being ignored in the face of someone you love glamouring strangers and others. Of accepting what's given—for too long. Not being seen. Not being chosen. Or being chosen for what you offer—not for who you are.

I remember the quiet panic as a child when it came time to choose partners at school. I was rarely picked first—unless it was for a sport. Then I was chosen because I was good. It continued into adolescence. Friend groups where I was included—but not fully present. At the time, I didn't dwell on it. I was busy—dance, sports, building something for myself. School was something I moved through, not something I anchored in. Long before it was over I was ready to move on.

But I always knew: I would create my own world. Find my people. Be understood—without needing to explain myself. And I have.

Looking back, I can see the patterns clearly. Subtle exclusion. Passive dynamics. The quiet ways people make space for themselves by pushing others out—something I experienced well into my late 20s, and sharply experienced once recently. Rejection is redirection. Every experience moved me forward—even when it didn't feel like it at the time.

In relationships, invisibility looked different—but it felt the same. Sitting at a bar with someone I was dating, only to have his attention drift elsewhere. Conversations happening around me—but not with me. Unacknowledged. Unchosen. There were moments I tried to prove myself. And moments I stopped—because it was exhausting.

Sometimes we don't have the strength to change it at the moment. Sometimes we believe it will shift if we try harder. I learned that connection doesn't work when only one person is fully there.

Today, I'm intentional about something simple: acknowledgment. Seeing people. Meeting them where they are. Letting them receive it. It goes further than anything else. No gift replaces presence. No gesture replaces being seen.

The Principle

There are many forms of love, but never the same love twice. Nothing moves us like it. It is the invisible thread that binds and breathes life into everything we create. When it's real, there is no denying it—try as you might. Not all love is meant to last a lifetime. Some arrive for a reason, some for a season, and some—for life. To become an expression of love is one of the greatest undertakings of a life. Real love creates calm. It is steady, consistent, and secure—not conditional, manipulative, or transactional. And like anything worth receiving, you must become it first. Love is an agreement. First with yourself, then with others.

I'll never forget hearing a friend's wedding vows. In 2012, at their home in Cabo, he said to her:

"Lacy, you are easy to love."

Those words hit me like a ton of bricks—as someone who grew up believing love was conditional. That it had to be earned. There is nothing hard about you to love. The real you will be adored for the very things someone else once held against you.

A Pivotal Command

In 2015, after the sudden loss of my mother, while in a relationship that had quietly eroded my worth, I heard a message as clearly as anything I've ever known:

"Become an expression of love."

It wasn't a suggestion. It was a command.

I didn't fully understand it, but I committed to it immediately. What snapped into focus was this: I always have me. No one is guaranteed. I am.

So tell people you love them. Don't wait. Mean it.

I'm content alone, and I love partnership—being a strong, committed team. Romantic love, when it's safe and reciprocal, is one of life's great gifts. Compatibility, values, and shared vision matter more than fleeting chemistry.

Not everyone has partnership etched into them—and that's okay. It's far easier to be in a relationship with someone who actually desires to be in one. And if you're ready for love, open the gates. Speak clean and clearly. Do not contradict your desire with doubt, or speak as though it's something you do not want. When the desire is honest, it becomes harder to ignore—and easier to recognize when it's met.

How Love Finds Us

Love has always come to me through friendship. Easily. Naturally. Never forced. Resisted, mostly. At the time, I didn't realize this was a pattern. I just thought it was how things were. It was easy to keep things light—until the next layer or level was required. I don't avoid depth—but I value freedom. I wanted it to stay easy. Uncomplicated.

I've been in long-term partnerships and brief

romances since I was young. All evolved me. Some humbled me. All taught me something essential. I don't have a "type." What's consistent isn't age or appearance—it's alignment. Vision, capacity, rhythm, heart.

We often attract who we are in the moment—and sometimes who we're ready to become. Relationships reveal what's alive in us at that time. What's unhealed. What's ready to grow. Are we moving in the same direction? Do our values align? Will we evolve together—or apart? That's the real question.

After my mother passed—and in the absence of safety—I learned this: when everything around you feels out of control, the only thing you can recalibrate is yourself. Fine-tune yourself, and the world begins to shift with you. You set the tone. I noticed how often fear reshaped the story in my head, and once I did, I started choosing love—which dissolved confusion and removed doubt.

On Changing Form

If a temporary love exits your life, let it drift. It's making space for something more real. Love meets you at the level you're able to receive it. Have you refined yourself to the depth required to receive what you desire? Life meets us where we are—and so do the people on our path. I've healed abandonment wounds so deep they once defined me. And I can tell you this: you can become safe, grounded, and deeply committed—without losing yourself, without suffocating anyone, without fear. Love is a gift. It is not a lifeline. Freedom exists within relationship as an expander—not a constraint.

Available For

Living with an open heart isn't the same as being unguarded. I've always been open to love as it arrives. Not chasing it. Not structuring my life around it. I've always had my own direction—dreams, goals, things that held my focus. Relationships were never the goal. They were a bonus—and something I love. A playmate for life—yes, sign me up.

After experiencing absence, chaos, and unpredictability, I realized the highs and lows weren't depth—they were instability. Exhausting. Unnecessary. What I came to value was calm. Peace. Safety—without drama. Steady companionship. A partner. A teammate. There's less adrenaline there—but more truth. A steady heartbeat. A clean flow. You can still have passion and adventure within the calm. It's completely possible.

I've experienced the other side. The kind of connection that keeps you slightly off-balance. Where you adjust yourself to absorb unpredictability. Where you accept inconsistency and walk on eggshells—or what I now recognize as conditional love. The kind that rewards performance. Good grades. Perfect behavior. Being compliant. Being chosen—as long as you don't fully be yourself—because that would be dangerous, disruptive or unacceptable for someone else. Of course nothing starts this way, but it can end up like this.

At some point, you recognize it. And once you do—you can't unsee it. The quiet cost of abandoning yourself to maintain a connection. And the realization that in a healthy relationship, that cost doesn't exist.

I remember sitting in my hairdresser Billy's chair one day, talking through all of this. It was our first time meeting, and we went deep quickly—as I often do with people who feel safe. We were talking about past relationships. What we had accepted. What we no longer would. That's when he said it: "Love scraps." It landed immediately. Because that's exactly what it was—receiving pieces, instead of presence. Attention in fragments. Care in doses. Enough to keep you there—but never enough to feel secure. I remember saying, without hesitation, I was no longer available for that. Not in theory—in reality. There was nothing anyone could offer me that would justify inconsistency. No apology that could compensate for a lack of presence. He laughed and said, "that's dangerous." He meant it as a compliment. Dangerous to anything built on control. Because once you see it clearly—control no longer works.

Side Note on Partnership

If there's one thing I've learned, how people manage stress —and time—matters. It shapes everything. I've seen how stress and time mismanagement break relationships. Before committing to partnership—especially one involving shared life or co-creation—notice how people relate to pressure, time, and possibility. Do they avoid, numb, or escape—or do they problem-solve, adjust, and stay present? Notice who "never has time," versus who creates it. Some search endlessly for reasons not to act. Others find one clear reason to say yes. These patterns repeat. I finally became clear about what I would—and wouldn't accept. Beliefs around love can change. Your nervous system always knows what feels safe, reciprocal, and real.

Betrayal Into Compassion

Betrayal is often treated as a black-and-white category. It's not. Context matters. Yes, I've experienced it. And this is not a way to live—so the only option is forward.

On either side of it—clarity matters more than reaction.

Understand what actually caused the breakdown. Feel the feelings—but don't dramatize the story. Betrayal doesn't always arrive like a hurricane. Sometimes it slips in quietly—through avoidance, neglect, or unmet needs. If it crossed your path, trust this: on some level, it arrived not as punishment, but as an expansion of your self-worth. See it clearly—and move forward.

The Relationship as Its Own Entity

I remember sitting next to a couple at Chow's in LA in 2011. I was on a date myself, and we struck up a conversation. Saturday was their date night. Exhausted? Stressed? Life unraveling just before? It didn't matter. That was the first time I witnessed commitment—not just to each other, but to the relationship itself. The relationship became something of its own. A third entity. A living thing to be honored and maintained. What you tend grows. What you neglect withers. Relationships are not meant for autopilot. Clarity creates safety. Communication creates ease.

Restoration

Even outside of long-term partnership, I've experienced moments of pure, unconditional love. Not loud. Not dramatic. Just present. Sweetness. Kindness. Connection. The kind that reveals itself in people who have lived—and come back softer, not harder. A quiet reminder that something real exists.

I'm grateful for my early imprints of love. They showed me what's possible—even when life didn't always reflect it. Playfulness. Care. The call to say you made it home—because they needed to know. Sometimes there are no words—just a feeling. And when that feeling returns—years later, in a different person—you recognize it immediately. A sense of safety. An exhale. Someone who sees you—and asks nothing of you. Consistency and acceptance. No demand to change. Nothing to prove. You fit—without needing to adjust yourself.

5
CHAPTER FIVE
FURRY VIPS

IT'S THEIR WORLD. We're just living in it.

Adventure

If these two had passports, they'd already need extra pages. So many miles. So many memories. These girls are ride-or-dies in every sense. Like me, the beach is their happy place—wind in their hair, sun on their faces. Planes, trains, automobiles, bikes—whatever corner of the world—they've never not been along for the ride.

And then there are the moments that remind you how fragile everything is. While living in St. Barts, we faced a medical emergency that couldn't be treated on the island. In a crisis, you learn a lot about where you live—and the island showed up. The local vet did what he could, providing Daisy's bloodwork and UA results.

We took the ferry to a neighboring island, where we were met by a calm, grounded visiting veterinarian from Trinidad. Her energy was heavenly—ridiculously calm.

My vibe. Celine Dion played softly as she treated Daisy, draining excess fluid from her belly. She patiently diagnosed her and brought Daisy back to a baseline I could manage until we eventually arrived months later in Miami for further testing.

Cue the girls' natural chef (me). Since then I've found an incredible local food service, but at the time—let's just say it was laborious. There's nothing I wouldn't do for them. When life is at stake, choices become clear instantly. Health—its presence or absence, snaps everything into focus. These girls are my family, my teachers, my mirrors, and the sweetest love bugs one could ask for—even when they are being mischievous. Cute cancels out naughty, in their case.

If you want to know who someone is, watch how they love an animal and their level of patience for them.

Their Selflessness

Animals are deeply intuitive beings, and sponges to our inner state. They bond deeply with us.

It wasn't until Daisy had her flare-up that something truly clicked for me. She wasn't just reacting physically—she was absorbing what was happening around me. The temporary situational post-traumatic stress living in my body at the time. A reflection of my environment. She was shielding me emotionally and energetically in the only way she knew how—absorbing it through her tiny four-pound body.

My understanding deepened years earlier when I briefly volunteered in the foster department at an LA dog rescue (shout out to HIT Living and Wishbone Rescue). I say "briefly"—five or six months, because it was intense.

While I'm resilient in the human realm, my capacity is far less resilient when it comes to animals. God bless the people who do this work every day.

The cases that came through were devastating: neglect, abuse, abandonment. Rage surfaced in me at how these animals had been treated. Many arrived not only physically ill, but with behavioral needs—not because they were "bad," but because they had absorbed chaos, fear, abuse, and instability for far too long. I won't list the cases or the subtle forms of neglect I witnessed—they break my heart too much knowing they happen quietly, everywhere. Just know that small shortcuts and subtle neglect ricochet. What moved me most was witnessing what happened next. Once these animals were nourished, acknowledged, and consistently cared for, something remarkable occurred. Health returned. Temperament softened. Trust re-emerged. Their little nervous systems stabilized. Just like us.

When we are properly seen, loved, and held in safety, the body remembers how to heal—and respond.

Love Over Sacrifice

On my walk today something came to me.

I've heard people express concern about having dogs—or even being in a relationship—because of the idea of sacrifice. But I don't really believe in sacrifice. I believe in choices. When love outweighs what is exchanged, sacrifice disappears.

6

CHAPTER SIX

TRAUMA AND THE BODYMIND

BEFORE POST-TRAUMATIC STRESS—CAUSED by a car accident, chronic relational stress, and six years of head-injury symptoms, I had a strong baseline. A steady core. That baseline became my internal reference point when everything else fell apart. It showed up as instinct—doing what came naturally to feel better across every area of my life.

Even with that reference point, reemerging from those states took everything I had. I used to wonder what my life would look like today had I not done the work beforehand—unwavering self-trust and body awareness that allowed me to repair, restore, and regenerate my vessel. It would not have been pretty.

Fine-tuning the body-mind is non-negotiable. It isn't a onetime thing. It's a practice—for life. The nervous system is chemical and electrical. It is far more adaptable than fragile. We are far more resilient than you'd think. When I realized this, I stopped outsourcing my power—relying on something else to do what my inner being is most capably equipped for. Pharmaceuticals attempt to rebalance chemistry from the outside. The body, however, has its own internal pharmacy. The work is learning how to access it. As someone who was on Adderall after the sudden death of my mother—only to wake up one day realizing I was no longer attuned to my core, I stopped cold turkey 3 years later. I prefer to be tapped into my senses as close to my natural reserve as possible. There is no right or wrong choice, there are only choices. Awareness matters.

Draw From and Transcend

There is a kind of power I eventually started accessing after working through this particular trauma—once I gained authority over it. A power that created an unshakeable core—and a low tolerance for lack luster behavior when I'd come upon it in the outside world.

Some things you don't forget: the broken glass, the airbags crashing into you, the sounds, the smells, the impact. The bystanders and the emergency responders. Phantom pain all crossing my chest. Who showed up—and who did not, years later. Who disappeared immediately. Who arrived without hesitation or question in the eleventh hour. Who lent their hand, their time, and their contacts. And who couldn't meet you where you were—because they didn't have the capacity to meet themselves. Some things we remember in order to keep our strength in perspective.

No matter the traumatic event or events that have added up over time—place yourself in another kind of moment —when the deepest cuts were words, and the impact landed in your chest like a ton of bricks. Repeatedly. That too, causes physical imprints and impact. Muscle memory absorbs and stores it. Record keeping.

I remember a time when sleep became my refuge and the only place I could catch my breath. Maybe you've been there. And then—something otherworldly happens: You realize you can draw from that internal reservoir without being owned by it.

You can alchemize an inner state into a completely different outward response when the moment calls for it. What once caused inner depletion is now an energy bank to cause and create. This is a strange gift that comes from surviving something you never thought you would. A car accident you shouldn't have walked away from alive. Abuse—in any form, of any kind—an era that required you to become someone else just to make it through. Defining moments that split your life into "before and after"—some of them growing so misty they no longer render memory at all. Deleted.

We do what we do to save ourselves—be it rewriting a memory, deleting it—or changing our state. Sometimes changing our states requires putting on a new character—but not the kind to fit in for acceptance purposes—the kind to live.

I remember a time where I would over-emote a different emotion to escape the painful emotion I was in. In moments like this, you do whatever it takes. Be you—but a different version. Override the current system. Change the internal response—change the outer picture. From anxious to calm. From needing to know to being completely at peace with not knowing. From emotionally taxed to mentally unavailable for nonsense. Think differently, be differently, create a different result. It really was that simple—during a season of short-term memory loss from head injury. When staying awake took incomprehensible effort. When sleep wasn't rest, but necessity. If you've been there, you know: sometimes all you can do is sleep.

During this time, it wasn't that I stopped being myself. It was that I chose to step into a version that could rise above my then-circumstances. One with focus and with command. Trauma does not get the final word. But you do have to decide when you're done living inside it. Suffering forces the choice. Commitment keeps you moving forward.

Self-Worth Is Your Safety

A healthy sense of embodied self-worth negotiates for you. An inner stability that is unshakeable—is more secure than any outside force that promises 'safety'. It is your resource and energy bank—your Source. It is the quiet, unshakable truth that you are worthy simply because you exist. Nothing to prove. No award to earn.

We are taught to outsource safety and worth—to people, outcomes, approval—until life eventually teaches us what cannot be taken away: these are not currencies to be traded. They are inherent. Freely given. It is not a matter of becoming—but of access. Of remembering.

Imagine placing your sense of safety in someone else's hands—offering it like precious crystal—only to watch it slip and shatter when you most need to feel held. When the glass hits the floor, the silence afterward is deafening. And in that silence, only one presence remains: you. You are the solid ground. Feel the beat of your heart: it's steady.

Your provision is not held by anyone's mood, approval, or capacity. Your provision is from God, the Creator—the Universe. Call it what is real for you.

I learned that safety is feeling secure in my body—when everything around me crumbled or vanished. When nothing external was stable—I had myself. Even when I felt unsafe to be seen and unsafe in my body—I knew I always had me, and if I was going to bet on anything—there is no question, it was going to be me.

When everything familiar disappears. You are the stability, not someone or something else. You are worthy—not because someone stayed, approved, or chose you—but because you are. That truth was written into your body before your first breath. When trauma enters the system, this foundation of worth and safety can shake—and that is not your fault. But it is your responsibility to realign it.

Be Nudged or Be Violently Shaken

The mind forgets, the body remembers. The call to change nudges before it shakes. Guidance arrives gently—until you can no longer ignore it. I refused to acknowledge my gut instincts. And instead, my body spoke for me: Cystic acne, hair loss, weight imbalance, ulcers, anxiety, cognitive fog, insomnia and more.

I had felt the nudges—and seen them. They were constantly interrupting my life. I knew what needed to change but fear froze me in motion—staying busy, but not truly living for myself. This is where many people get suspended in time: going through the motions like a machine, but not choosing with honesty. Ignore guidance long enough, and life intervenes. Illness starts in the mind. What rises as fear is often pain that has not yet been metabolized. The mind protects us by suppressing what we are not ready to face—until the body insists.

If something surfaces, know this: you already have the capacity to meet it—and it is ready to be met. Some truths rise slowly—through rest, through sleep, through the subconscious, in deep rest. That is where my own healing began. More on that later.

Energy Economics

Trauma—large or small—is unfinished emotion stored in the body. Something happened too fast, too intensely, or without support to process it—and the body-mind never completed the cycle. The memory loops until a new pattern interrupts it. It is energetically expensive to live this way—and it is not longevity-friendly. It ages you from the inside out.

You have an energy bank—mental, physical, emotional, spiritual. Every day includes withdrawals and deposits. I had a clear awareness and still do—of how I was spending this. Living with post traumatic stress, energy leaks often go unnoticed. Background programs you never consciously agreed to keep running—draining vitality, focus, creativity, and joy. Keeping you separate from what you truly want. Distracted instead of focused.

For a long time, I appeared high-functioning. Inside, I was scraping an empty barrel. A better than full recovery and healing journey began the moment I stopped managing symptoms and got real about what was at the root.

Humility and Power

Trauma commands humility. This is the opposite of weakness. It is grounded through awareness and powerful surrender. True humility lives in your bones. It's not a something you do or are once in a while. It softens ego without erasing it completely. Humility allows all parts of you to be present—calm, clear, certain—to communicate confidently without saying a word. It refines personal power, and does not demand commentary. There is nothing loud about this type of subtle inner authority, but the vast ripple is beyond measure.

Shout Out

This is an acknowledgment to those who respond in the face of trauma. After my accident, my compassion for first responders deepened in a way I hadn't known before. The day after the accident, I went to retrieve my computer from my Range Rover—eighty percent written off, metal twisted and collapsed. I was still shaken (for years to come), but physically intact. The woman helping me paused and asked, "Who was driving?" I said, "Me." Her face shifted from confusion to horror.

One of my closest friends is married to a firefighter. He wasn't on shift when my accident happened, but he heard about it. Over time, I've heard stories of scenes he's responded to—images I would never want to witness. The witnessing alone leaves an imprint. And if it isn't worked through, it lodges itself inside, manifesting just as trauma does for those directly impacted. I know this because I've been there. What isn't processed doesn't disappear; it redirects and will surface in behavior when you least expect it.

I'll never forget watching a scene in Mad Men. Don Draper's character walks into the home of his former wife to see her sitting on the sofa—at which time she told him she had cancer. That moment took me back to my mother on her sofa—our last goodbye. A mirror image replicated and felt. That scene, prompted a stream of tears. Trauma doesn't discriminate by role. Witnessing counts. Healing is essential to our health and to evolving ourselves.

No matter your position in a traumatic event, if it reaches you at the core, it changes you. It sharpens awareness of how fragile life is—how precious each human body—and soul, truly is.

Draw From Others' Miracles

This could live in the body chapter, but it belongs here. It is directly tied to my recovery from head injury—and to how trauma transforms when it's met with deeply convicted belief.

If one person on this earth has made a better-than-full recovery from something—anything—so can you. Years later, I came across research confirming what I had already discovered in my own recovery: belief changes physiology. I share this because you need to know: healing is available for you. If someone else has achieved, created, or become something—you can too. That belief has lived in me since childhood: If they're doing it, so can I.

After my accident, I had several things working in my favor: muscle memory, an understanding of how to move and nourish my body, self-awareness, emotional intelligence—and perhaps most importantly, example.

Rewinding to my twenties, I was once in a relationship with an athlete whose sport was aggressive and high-impact. He suffered a catastrophic injury that left him paralyzed and in a coma for months. Doctors were unsure what—if anything—would return. He rehabilitated through relentless visualization and physical therapy. Morphine was used initially in the hospital, but once the acute phase passed, his father intervened. He did not want his son dependent on anything that dulled awareness or slowed healing. Despite multiple broken bones and immense pain, there was no long-term reliance on pharmaceuticals. They made him foggy. He did, however, use cannabis intentionally—to manage inflammation and arthritic pain. He was precise, conscious, and disciplined about this. There were no chemicals in his food. Sugar was limited. Alcohol was minimal to nonexistent.

What I learned through observing him was this: pain lives in the mind far more than we're told—and food is either medicine or poison. I had witnessed this from my grandmothers, but seeing someone live it with such rigor made it undeniable. Non-negotiable.

We are always being given what we need—even if we don't realize it until decades later. Some relationships may not last but they do carry profound teachings. That one gave me a living blueprint for recovery—years before I ever needed it.

During my own recovery from head injury and post traumatic stress, I conducted over two hundred formal interviews with people living with similar conditions. I wanted to hear first hand their struggles and how they lived. I wanted the details. I asked structured questions. I looked for patterns. The differentiator was clear and almost always immediate: belief—and environment. Did the person believe they could fully recover, or had they been told a story of limitation? Were they surrounded by people who reinforced possibility—or fear? I had an example to draw from—and have questioned that which has needed questioning since childhood. Not everyone did. And my recovery reflected that difference. Additionally, three words: sun, fresh air and sleep. Mega contributors to recovering. Recovery is not mystical—although it can be miraculous. What it is, is patterned. The patterns are visible if you are willing to look.

There was another experience that reinforced this truth for me. In 2015, on a Sunday in New York City, I attended an event at abc carpet & home. The speaker lineup was exceptional—Gabby Bernstein, Hannah Bronfman, Tata Harper, and Dr. Mario Martinez among them.

Dr. Martinez shared a study involving two groups. One group was guided to relive their glory days—their vitality, strength, and aliveness. The other group was repeatedly reminded of their frailty and decline. Long-term outcomes followed the story each group was fed—measured later in health and longevity.

I remember thinking, Is it really that simple?

Yes. The story impacts us that much.

Takeaway: mind your inputs.

What you consume.
Who you listen to.
What you believe is possible.
Input creates outcome—in every domain.

Standing Invitation

You are not defined by what happened to you. Trauma is not a life sentence unless you decide to make it one. You can release it. You can transform it—and live differently. Decide what you want. Refine who you choose to be. Treat yourself with the love and respect you once reserved for others. Trauma may leave a scar, but it does not own you. The body is self-healing. Identity can be recalibrated. Decide who you are—and live accordingly.

7
CHAPTER SEVEN
SHAME

Shame is one of the heaviest emotions a human being can carry. It can feel like an anchor between where you are and where you want to be. The feeling is real. The idea that it's permanent is not. Shame asks to be acknowledged—not carried like a life sentence. It asks to be understood and released. What remains useful reveals itself. The rest falls away. Think of it like an old boarding pass from a flight that already landed. The journey is over. The receipts are no longer required.

For a long time, I lived in reference to my accident. I saw it as a setback that delayed the life I was building. When I reframed the situation, the trajectory of my life changed. What once felt like pushing a boulder uphill began to feel like opening a door and letting the current rush in. Frustration into flow. At its most useful, shame is not an identity. It is a catalyst. And you always have the power to make something else of it.

The Shame Bubble

Shame lives like a sealed bubble. Pressurized, self-contained, quietly shaping your emotional state and behavior. Inside it live old narratives, inherited beliefs, other people's projections, and unprocessed moments. See them clearly. Then release the grip. The bubble breaks—and you breathe again.

Consequence versus Captivity

During my recovery from a head injury, I sentenced myself to time. I had lost my license after receiving a distracted-driving ticket. The entire event carried shame, but losing my license affected me more than I expected. My identity had always been tied, in some small way, to having a beautiful car. Looking back, the question revealed something deeper. Who was I without the car? Who was I without the things I had lost? Until I began rebuilding my life piece by piece, shame was where my non-existent car was parked.

Back to captivity—I believed I needed to pay for the shame—to suffer long enough for it to be earned away. I carried it everywhere. I wore it like penance. I thought responsibility meant punishment. Responsibility is real and integrity matters, but self-punishment does not heal. Healing comes through reconciliation—through grace, through choice.

One day something clicked—not dramatically, but decisively. I saw that the shame I was carrying wasn't only about the accident. It was layered with everything beneath it: old identities, quiet self-judgments, agreements I had never renegotiated. Awareness turns the key. Choice opens the door. Had I understood that sooner, I would have lived differently. Still—no regrets. I could not be more grateful for my life today; every event led me to right now.

Shame Frequency and the Fog

Shame is like a dense fog that you don't even realize you are in. It changes how you walk into a room, how you make eye contact, it distorts perception, it narrows your field of view. When you're in it, it is difficult to see clearly. Decisions feel harder than they need to be. Movement feels delayed. Fortunately, shame is a state of being, and states of being can be changed.

Speak It or Carry It

Speaking it out loud loosens shame's chokehold. Tell one human who doesn't flinch when they hear it. This does not require a detailed confessional on the internet—but if that's your thing, go for it. We don't judge around here; we hold space for and accept. In my experience, when shame finally comes out, the tension breaks instantly and full body relief sets in.

Visible Shame

Some shame is loud, public, and obvious. I remember the millisecond of impact—the slow-motion flash where time fractured. The sentence that repeated in my head as I was helped out of my upside-down vehicle was simple: This is terrifying. But I'm alive. This is the upside. Forever grateful.

From the outside, I looked fine. No broken bones. No visible scars. Inside, my nervous system was frozen in shock. I couldn't stand in a grocery store—the lights felt too bright. The ping of a text message made every hair on my body stand up. Shame doesn't always show up with bruises. Sometimes it embeds itself quietly—reshaping behavior, tone, energy—long before the mind has language for it.

For years, I carried a heavier aura than I ever had. I carried imagined judgment like bricks on my chest. What I eventually understood was this: Even then—even at my lowest—opportunity and incredible beings still found me. I was internally prepared even at rock bottom—I never stopped doing the work—even when the results weren't immediately reflected before my eyes. It does catch up. Luck is truly a byproduct of preparedness, it doesn't just happen.

Invisible, Atomic Shame

Not all shame is situationally explosive. Some of it infiltrates quietly. Invisible shame is subtle. It disguises itself as personality, as perfectionism, as shrinking back and calling it "protection." It hides in hyper-achievement, people-pleasing, quiet self-denial. It arrives through small moments: Passing comments, misaligned environments, words that land at exactly the wrong time. Individually, they seem insignificant, together, they shape identity.

I once had someone casually comment on what they found most attractive in women—naming physical ethnic traits I could never embody. It wasn't meant to be cruel.

But something sharp lodged itself inside me. That frequency no longer registers. Once I recognized it, it stopped shaping me. The narratives, the people and your environment shapes you. Clear vision parts the fog.

Alignment, Duplicity, and Worthiness Leaks

I noticed something: every time I said yes when I meant no, something in me split. When your heart says one thing, your words say another, and your actions follow neither, something fractures internally. I noticed ways I had been behaving in duplicity:

- Staying where you've already outgrown
- Entertaining what you know doesn't work
- Tolerating crumbs and calling it patience

Discomfort rose every time I stayed where I knew I didn't belong. Something in me dimmed and contracted. Not dramatically. Just slightly. Enough to feel it—and bit by bit move further away from who I was. When I stopped gripping what was never mine to carry forever, something else returned—clarity, and dignity. Shame was never my identity, despite it feeling so for a season.

8

CHAPTER EIGHT

GUIDANCE

YOUR LIFE DOES NOT HAVE limits. You are the architect.

i. DON'T DELAY. Start before needing guarantees or a detailed plan. The next step appears when you need it.
ii. THERE ARE NO MISTAKES. Rejection is protection and redirection. Every negative can glean a positive.
iii. YOU HOLD THE KEYS. Fine tune the bodymind to tap into the guidance of your reliable, trustworthy inner compass—your heart.
iv. HONESTY WITH SELF CHANGES EVERYTHING. A truthful decision paired with action rearranges destiny.
v. YOU CAN HANDLE IT. You are resourced. You are creative. Get brave.
vi. FAITH LOVES THE FEARLESS. Faith responds to courage. Love dissolves fear. Every decision

routes you closer to or further from what you want.

vii. TAKE THINGS FOR FACE VALUE. Energy is ultimate read and how your body responds.

viii. ACKNOWLEDGE OTHERS. Be vulnerable. Say what you mean in the moment.

ix. ALLOW PEOPLE TO SUPPORT YOU. Asking is a sign of strength not a weakness.

x. LIFE IS A MIRROR. Your inner world is expressing on the outside.

xi. YOU EXIST INSIDE THE PARADIGM YOU'VE EITHER CREATED OR ACCEPTED. What you allow will continue. And, your environment and the company you keep—very much matter.

xii. SIMPLICITY IS POWER.

xiii. GOD MAKES UP FOR 'LOST' TIME, although time, is but an illusion.

xiv. CONSISTENCY IS A FORM OF LOVE when it's freely given. This is among the most safe forms of love.

xv. THE SIMPLE, NATURAL, DIVINELY GUIDED THING IS THE THING. Worthy as you are now. Nothing more to add. The most powerful impact often comes from the most simply translated and not from the complicated.

xvi. GET UP AND GET READY FOR THE DAY EVERYDAY.

xvii. PRACTICING AND LIVING THE LAWS OF (NON) AND (SELF) YIELDS IDEAL HEALTH, AND A NATURAL RHYTHM AND CYCLE OF GIVING AND RECEIVING.

   - NON VIOLENCE: we are all one. Do unto others as you would have done unto you is real. Think twice before causing harm through thought, words and action.

- Non resistance: the art of allowing. Allow what's meant to go—go, and get yourself into a state of allowing what's meant to reach you-reach you. Attune your bodymind ongoing to become nonresistant. This creates a natural state of flow.
- Non reactivity: mindfulness, in a nutshell. Temper your emotions through self awareness and choose how you respond. Non reactivity isn't just through interaction with others, it's in the ways we make choices that impact ourself–especially through how we treat our body.
- Non attachment: learning commitment and desire without attachment, knowing that all is always as its meant to be, will set you free.
- Self respect: your younger self, older self, and self tomorrow. How you treat yourself in this moment impacts all versions of yourself. We teach others how to treat us, often through how we treat ourselves.
- Self responsibility: in all areas of life. Ownership of what you are causing and creating–and ownership of your present circumstances. Be accountable for the past–reconcile, rewrite, heal and create a new to create a better present and future result. Take back any blame you've placed on another–and remember the part you played. Take back your power.
- Self love : being a loving expression in the world is what creates harmony. Love based

actions. Reconcile any distaste you have with yourself and see the good. Be grateful for this vessel you get to do life with and squeeze the juice out of all you have access to–be resourceful with what you have; appreciate and be grateful–and God will give you more to work with.

xviii. Everything, and everyone is your teacher.

xix. Love is always the answer.

PART II: AWAKEN

PERCEPTION AND CHOICE

1
CHAPTER ONE
THERE'S NOTHING WRONG WITH YOU

Reduce The Friction

YOUR SOUL already knows what's true—and knows the way. And there has never been anything wrong with you. Sometimes there's simply friction in the way. Reducing friction has always been one of my favorite activities. Translation: creating harmony.

From a young age I began removing small sources of friction in my life—the weather (choose where you live), work environments, daily attire—simple things that influence how a day unfolds. Align closer to what feels good by reducing friction. Less friction—fewer complaints, more harmony, more ease, more pleasant outcomes. Deny what you know you want and friction remains. The more aligned you are with your core, the more clearly you hear the guidance that was always meant for you.

Guidance supports decisions—and you make more decisions in a single day than you could ever count. The body is an intelligent guide. Access is always available.

In my darkest moments I leaned heavily on my relationship with God—and on fine-tuning my body-mind. These practices became stabilizers, bringing clarity when everything else felt uncertain.

Calm the noise, tune in, listen. The power and answers are there for your access on command.

Honesty With Self

When you tell the truth about what you want—without duplicity, life begins to move with greater ease. Things start falling into place. Truth is a feeling: stable, grounded, clear. The more clear you become, the easier it is to recognize the guidance meant for you—the quiet signals that were always present but easy to miss—or misinterpret; when life becomes loud and distracting.

Words Carry Weight

Words carry weight. Read the room—but/and, say what you mean in the first place. When you speak truthfully, your words land with power. When truth bends, the signal weakens and life detours. You may notice moments when you weren't honest about what you wanted—when you chose something safer, easier, or more acceptable—and life rerouted you entirely. And still the original desire remained, quietly waiting. Truth has a different quality to it: clean, simple, unmistakable. Sometimes a single honest sentence changes everything. Words ripple outward. Their weight becomes impact.

A Daily Declaration

My first boss in the investment industry, when I was twenty-three, used to walk into the office each morning with his incredible wife and declare:

"I am absolutely fabulous." At first I thought—really? Every day? Then I realized: yes. It was a choice. A declaration that shifted the energy of the room before the day even began. Words meant. Words spoken. Words backed by decision. That moment will stay with me forever.

Recalibration, Not Repair

The micro creates the macro. You are whole—even in the midst of chaos. You are not broken. You may simply need recalibration. Like a drained battery. Like a treasured instrument that needs tuning. Like precious cargo, arriving where it's meant to perfectly on-time. Not late to the party. If you ever feel shattered—even a little—remember: this too shall pass, often more quickly than you expect once you allow it.

Adjust the Lens

Sometimes life simply requires an adjustment of the lens. What first appears as rejection, loss, or an unfavorable outcome begins to soften when you understand this: It's either this—or something better. Equal to or greater than, always. It doesn't mean you were wrong. It simply means something wasn't right for you; a redirection, powerful protection. A path guiding you closer into alignment.

Your Internal Compass

We are all born with an internal compass—an invisible map housed within the walls of the heart. Yet most of us are taught to override it. The logical brain and intellect are extraordinary tools, but intelligence becomes a liability when it overrides intuition—when theory becomes more convincing than what you feel to be true. There is thinking. And there is feeling. One is fast. One is slow. Over time, the more I trusted myself, the less weight I placed on theory alone. Guidance was already present—I simply had to listen.

Your Energetic Signature

The light in your eyes—or the absence of it. Magnetic, calm, joyful—or heavy, disconnected, withdrawn. When you recognize the value of your life, you stop wasting time. You speak from the heart. You treat people as the precious beings they are. You move through your days with greater awareness. Your life is not infinite. But the way you choose to live it is entirely yours.

An Invitation

Let the contents of this book wash the dust of life away—like a hot shower at the end of a long day—as you step more fully into who you really are. I'm not going to tell you who you are. You decide. This book is partially memoir and partially transmission—but it is not about me. It is for you. Glean from my experiences. See differently, think differently, choose differently, move differently. Life moves quickly when decisions come from truth. Not perfectly, not cautiously, but truthfully. Everything unfolds in its own timing when you trust yourself from the inside out. And mistakes are fine. There really are no mistakes. We learn—and keep going.

Domino Effect

Time is respect. Respect gives rise to freedom. Quality decisions create quality time—and quality time is love. We are all simply learning how to live. You choose the ingredients of your life. You choose the characters who share it with you. If something feels off, trust yourself enough to change it rather than remaining stuck in confusion. Confusion keeps you circling. Clarity moves you forward.

Eventually I realized the answers I was searching for were already within me. When you attune the body-mind, the heart unlocks. We are all one. I am no better or worse than anyone—I simply am. So are you. Control is largely an illusion. God—the Creator, the Universe, whatever name you choose—is already moving the larger pieces. Your choice is simple: Co-create in truth and love—

or resist it.

2

CHAPTER TWO

FAITH AND THE DIVINE

To Each Their Own

I've come to believe much of life is in God's hands. I am no expert in this domain. I simply know what I know and share my experience. And I'm clear about what I subscribe to. What I hold is a drawing of values from multiple traditions that ultimately resolve into one fundamental idea: oneness. Unbeknownst to me, during the height of my recovery in 2018—after my head injury, post-traumatic stress, and a complete recalibration of self—I was instinctively living Kabbalistic principles. When the noise quiets, what we need tend to arrive exactly when we need it—whether we realize what it is, or whether we can name it. That's not what it's about. Clarity appears when distraction dissolves.

As with all things in this book, to each their own. Spirituality is deeply personal. It looks different for everyone. Think of belief systems like items on a menu. You don't have to order everything. Choose what resonates with you. I also tip my hat to A Course in Miracles, which entered my life in 2012. Its premise is simple and powerful: choose love over fear. That alone can guide every decision without requiring you to untangle complexities you may not yet be ready for.

One thing I've always appreciated about my upbringing is this: I was free to choose what I believed. Catholic grandparents who attended church. Parents who did not. For a town of about two thousand people, we had five or six different congregations. As someone observing this growing up, there was space for curiosity. Curiosity paired with respect matters. It always has for me. That foundation remains—so long as one principle stays intact: Do no harm.

Come to God Moments

The path of least resistance is alignment—feeling good, not forcing outcomes. When life becomes too heavy to carry alone, ask God to step in. Not from a place of begging or fixing, but from partnership. Doing life together. Faith is simply a willingness to be guided. When that relationship becomes real, life unfolds softer. Things feel lighter—because they are.

As a Child

When I was younger, I wanted a relationship with God—deeply—but I wasn't buying everything that was being sold. I grew up attending Catholic school. I loved the ritual of it, the reverence. If you grew up Catholic, the scent of incense never leaves you, nor does the sound of hymns sung and that big organ playing along. I still appreciate sacredness in many cultures—and in everyday life; care, intention, God is in the details. But beyond the ritual, I had questions. And no one could answer them in a way that felt true for me. So I stayed curious. I explored, listened, and walked my own version of a spiritual path.

My true come-to-God moment didn't arrive until 2019—when my circumstances became too much for any earthly control of my own. I was literally on my knees. And I asked for help. What I know now is simple: God lives in everything and in everyone. We are co-creators with Source—the Creator, the Divine—whatever name feels true to you.

There are ways of being that bring you into alignment with that truth. I had always been spiritual. But it wasn't until my mid-thirties that my relationship with God became real. If you desire a relationship with the Divine—whatever form that takes—it is available for you. When I began speaking to God directly, something shifted. Perhaps the most important thing I've learned is this: a relationship with God works best when it exists in all moments, not just in moments of crisis. Consistency creates the miracle. It dissolves anxiety and reminds you that far more is possible than you once believed.

Faith versus Control

Surrender does not mean giving up. It is not sitting on your hands or throwing in the towel. Surrender is releasing your plan and remaining open to the divine one. God's plan. Every time I tried to control outcomes—manipulate timelines, override intuition—the result was the same: Resistance, exhaustion, eventual collapse. Even when control worked temporarily, it was unsustainable. Faith creates breathing room. Control compresses everything into a box. When you are guided by God, the path reveals itself in ways you could never strategize—often with far more ease and far less pain.

Over time I learned to ask, listen, and watch for cues. Energy is a cue. What energizes you, what drains you. As adults, many of us are conditioned to look for proof instead of practicing faith. Faith can feel intangible. Many people trust only what they can see. But living purely in logic is far harder. Logic moves slowly. Faith bends time. When faith settles into the body—not just the mind—choices change. Energy shifts. Life reorganizes—not instantly, but undeniably. Trust the unfolding. Ask. Listen. Keep moving forward. One step, day, and thing at a time.

Deciding for a Divine Relationship

I've always been drawn to the unseen. The quiet knowing. The intuitive pull. The subtle instructions that arrive without words. Some arrive through pain, some through healing, some through being, some through relentless kindness. All of it counts. Flexibility and curiosity creates room for growth.

No Judgment

I've learned that spirituality isn't an aesthetic. Kindness, humility, and curiosity matter far more than labels.

Prayer

A few simple practices transformed my relationship with God. Throughout the day, I ask for guidance. I often ask for the next step to be revealed. Daily, I ask to be used for the highest good. In the quiet hours of the morning, before the world wakes up, I give thanks—not only for what exists, but for what has not yet arrived. Gratitude spoken in the present tense. I don't pray like a beggar. At night, I ask for purification of heart. I ask to be moved toward what serves—and gently removed from what harms. Eyes closed, hand resting on my chest, feeling the beat of my heart. It feels like dropping into a meditation you don't want to leave—a quiet synchronization. Deep connection. It took me decades to find this rhythm, and I'm deeply grateful for it. Faith is not for the faint of heart. Mine is tested often. But faith moves mountains where logic cannot.

You Are a Flow Through

God works through each of us, and each of us is a demonstration of the gifts we are given from God. We translate what's within—without. It's up to us to attune, develop, share, evolve, and expand. Do good in the word —in whatever way, and yes, naturally the return is a reward in some form. There was a time I felt shame around having nice things—because I was made to feel this way. Should my having create someone else's having not? No. But the energy was bad around the topic. This is not a thought or conversation that remotely enters my orb anymore. Life isn't about possessions—it's about people and experiences—and, we don't have to live like martyrs pretending we don't enjoy beauty, comfort, or well-made things, and being able to be generous. Good cookware, good sheets, our favorite textiles, a peaceful home to live, host and receive those we love, comfortable transportation that brings us joy, not to mention all things that allow our health—and the health of those we love. And experiences! Experiences—expand us. The list is endless. Money freedom often creates time freedom—and choice. And time is one of life's greatest luxuries. Money creates speed and access. Everything created on earth moves through us. So glorify God. Be useful. Let things unfold. And appreciate the beauty that exists in whatever form you encounter it. You are not doing this alone.

Courage and Perseverance

Courage bridges what faith begins. Fear will negotiate with your choices every single day. Let discomfort move through you. Choose from truth—not panic, fear, or scarcity. Move toward the life you want, even if you are wobbly and the path looks unreasonable from the outside. There's no such thing as safety—aside from the safety we create within ourself. Stagnation is often strategy frozen by fear. What I've come to realize is that you nor I am never alone, and this in itself—has removed anxiety that once debilitated me should I spend too much time solo. To move forward into the unknown is an act of faith. Keep going.

God Has Your Back

There are moments in life where outcomes cannot be explained by effort or chance alone. One of those moments for me was my accident in 2018. There was a split second before the worst part—a millisecond that rearranges your life forever. If you've lived through something that should have taken you out, you know that moment. Time suspends, there is a distinct sound that permeates the ears—and something deeper reveals. Eyes closed, I said out loud: Help me. I know I was met and protected; a legion of angels intervened. Near-death experiences—even these, we negotiate unconsciously. It's wild how much eternity fits inside a single millisecond. Another reminder that time may not be as real as we think. Consciousness is.

Operating as Your Higher Self

I am not perfect. Not even close. I walk imperfectly every day. I make mistakes, I reflect, adjust, and continue forward. The goal is not flawlessness. The intent is moving into closer alignment and improving a little more each day. Incremental gains—with grace. I began asking myself a simple question:

What would the steady, grounded version of me choose?—the version of me that exists where today's stresses are no longer, and where positive overflow is present? What does she feel like, what does life look like? What simply does not matter—that might be magnified today?

The higher self doesn't panic. It doesn't react impulsively. It knows things tend to work out—and it moves accordingly. Love-based or fear-based? Truth or ego? That question alone has saved me years. We do the best we can with the information we have—and then we refine. Faith doesn't mean you won't stumble, or doubt yourself. It means you won't walk alone, and that it's all going to be okay.

3
CHAPTER THREE
THE INTELLIGENT BODY

Infinite Intelligence and Self Healing

When you listen to the body, it will guide you. It is your instrument. I fine-tune the body-mind the way some people brush their teeth—by second nature habit. I grew up dancing competitively, which meant years in front of mirrors—fueled by comparison. It was the 90s. Later I lived inside of concussion. Six years of neurological interruption. Hyper-vigilance. Not knowing it. One fact held constant: the body is always communicating. Healing begins with listening. Then applying. Trial and error. Feedback. What is required is self-trust—inner authority that is not outsourced. Not copying someone else's protocol. Not moving through life sedated, repeating patterns that erode you. Routine is lovely, but flexibility and adaptability is power. The nervous system is a chemical cocktail. When it's regulated, you stop looking outward for rescue. Call it self-healing, coherence, or remembering.

The Body

Time shows up on the body. As does truth. What is heavy—shows up. Shed the emotional toxicity—it's the weight and inflammation stuck to you. The guilt, the shame, the baggage. Return to the elements that have always known how to heal you:

The warmth of the sun.

Salty, heavy sea air.

Sand on the body.

Earth under the feet.

Twinkling night stars as a heavenly blanket.

There was a season I never looked better. It was a by-product of my daily life. Structure without rigid routine. Boatloads of fruit. I was still working at this time—with plenty of core foundational and fundamental uncertainty. Nothing was perfect. I couldn't wait around for perfect. I dialed into the next twelve months—showed up, did the details, released what I'd outgrown. God's plan. I do my part. A beautiful life can be a beautiful distraction. But a nourished one shows on your face.

Listening

Fasting for me, albeit more rare than I'd like, is more about silencing the food-body than discipline. The summer of St. Tropez I started doing grape fasts—and felt a euphoric surge of energy. This grape euphoria journey was inspired by my dear friend Nina, a Côte d'Azur woman herself. I was still having cacao. Still accepting a couple of tea biscuits from my concierge angels, Cyril and Salomé. I was still living my life. But the volume shifted. When the noise drops, truth rises. And truth rarely enters politely. It can feel like anxiety before it feels like clarity. Like exposure before it feels like power. Silence does it. This is when the body begins to speak—not dramatically, not loudly, but clearly. What becomes apparent becomes undeniable.

The discomfort most people attribute to hunger is rarely hunger. It's proximity to themselves. It's the sudden awareness of everything they've been buffering with food, scrolling, gossip, productivity, noise. Most people don't fear deprivation. They fear capacity. When I stopped sedating myself with distraction, something sharpened. My body's signals grew precise. My energy steadied. Decisions simplified. The body does not whisper forever. Eventually, it begs. When you love and respect it—not obsessively, but reverently, it responds. It shape shifts, energy stabilizes. Behavior aligns—and alignment creates inner authority.

Poison in Plain Sight

The toxins of modern life are rarely hidden—they're normalized. In the water that runs from the tap. By the way, we need water that's alive. Not water that is stripped of minerals. Extract the chemicals, keep the minerals. More toxins hidden and normalized—in ultra-processed foods marketed as healthy, even at the health stores. In the products we put on our skin. The body is permeable. It absorbs much more than we think. What runs in the background seeps in. What and who touches your skin matters—the energy and biochemical makeup of others. What you feed your mind matters most of all—it's awareness.

After my head injury, I would speak to my body out loud. When you live any trauma to the body, parts of the body can turn phantom. Disconnected, desensitized, dissociated. A specific oil on my skin. Copper dry brush. Gua Sha. Words spoken aloud. I loved my body more than ever. I was grateful it was in one piece. I started to notice how beautiful it really was—I was. I was putting myself back together—energetically and with physical touch. My body came back online not because I forced it. Because I genuinely loved and respected it. Less is more. Ease over force. Results shape shift when there's air to breathe.

Alcohol

Alcohol, technically, is not ideal for the body. And yet—I appreciate a beverage given the right moment; albeit rare over the course of the past 10 years. There is a difference between appreciation and escape. In my twenties, alcohol blurred feelings I wasn't yet conscious of, ready to acknowledge or see. It felt like connection and sometimes it was. I genuinely had a lot of fun. It just got to a point where I looked in the mirror one day and realized the overindulgence—was slowing me down, aging me, and I didn't love my personality at times. That's all since taken new form, and a different energy. Overconsumption of anything carries a distinct energetic signature. Today I choose the time and place—sparingly, and when the moment strikes. Nothing calculated, nothing forced. An at the moment choice.

Different Bodies

Work with what you've got not against. Flow vs force. Love vs hate. Psychology shapes physiology more than we admit. I have mentally shape-shifted my body more than once. Thighs, arms, face, hair. When belief aligns with action, matter reorganizes. Acceptance precedes change, force resists it. Different DNA. Different chemistry. Different terrain. What inflames one body heals another. Your body is not a group project. Observe, adjust, refine, repeat. Trust intuition as much as science. Neither needs to dominate the other.

Burnout or Traumatic Stress Body

When the nervous system has endured physical trauma, concussion, or prolonged stress, the baseline shifts. Homeostasis changes, cognition slows. Memory feels distant until you work it like a muscle. Signals misfire. You become unreceptive—not because you're unwilling, but because you're surviving. With a head injury, you know it. With burnout, you often don't. Burnout is a quiet fog—a muted, zombified state where even "healthy" choices become reactive because thinking itself is exhausting. Grief does this too. So does post-traumatic stress. I've lived all of them—and recovered. With a head injury, nourishment is non-negotiable. With burnout, excess "healthy" carbs and sugars quietly derail metabolism. With grief, you can forget to eat entirely—mentally vacating the body. Awareness is the turning point. Once I saw what was happening, I chose differently—not from obsession, but from honesty. Your body is a bank account. Your habits are deposits or withdrawals.

During my head injury recovery, my brain needed healthy fats every morning. My body didn't want coffee—but it could tolerate Earl Grey or chai. I only craved what I needed. Energy was limited, so food became fuel—input for output. What surprised me most was how past knowledge resurfaced. Old habits, recipes, sensory memory. Muscle memory is real—not just for movement, but for emotion. Feelings live in the fibers of the body. Releasing what's stored there can heal the system as powerfully as food—sometimes more.

Living with traumatic stress, or the energy demands of a brain injury, teaches you quickly: there is only so much in the tank. I remember needing to rest before and after showering. Only being able to do one "big thing" a day. Being afraid to travel because I didn't know if I'd have enough energy to make it to my destination. Being afraid I'd never again live at the pace I once did. Regaining that energy has been one of the greatest blessings of my life. Sleep healed my body and brain. Sunshine healed them further—and I swear it's the thing that gave me back my energy. Food matters—but these come first. Input versus output.

During all of these states—head injury, burnout, grief—I did not have access to endless appointments, testing, or ideal resources. I worked with what I had. I trusted myself. I got the job done. What is required is honesty. The body is self-healing by design.

Sex and the Body

Everything in this realm is vibration. Sex can be consumption—or divine communion. Connection, nourishment and beauty—or transaction. Spiritual, or simply for pleasure. None of this is inherently wrong. The body knows the difference. Your body is precious and sacred. Especially here. For those carrying unprocessed trauma in the body, sex can sometimes become a form of numbing or escape disguised as closeness. Union rooted in truth, intention, respect, and care evolves the soul. It expands the aura, it heightens your vibration, it deepens your relationship with life itself. This is sacred ground. The body knows.

Safety and Power

The world trains us to seek safety outside ourselves. In people. In jobs. In relationships. In predictability. Security placed in external sources—things you cannot actually control—becomes outsourced safety. And once you see it that way, you realize how much anxiety is baked into that model. Society often frames these external measures as "security." Stability. Reliability. Sometimes there is value there, but in my experience, it can also become a gilded cage. I learned this the hard way—when everything I had placed my safety in fell apart. My first corporate job, where I was thriving, ended abruptly. A relationship I believed was forever altered my career path. And the deepest rupture of all: believing the security of automatically given love itself was guaranteed through my mother—until she died. Each time, what I thought was safety was revealed to be conditional.

So why is this in the body chapter? Because I learned the truth of safety when I had nothing but myself—inside the fog of concussion and post-traumatic stress. After physical trauma, I didn't just feel emotionally shaken. I felt unsafe inside my body. Unsafe to be seen. Having lost my voice—disjoined, my brain thought faster than my words could come out, and often I was simply speechless. Stripped of executive functioning—which stunted my quality of life in basic needs. Only when I rebuilt safety internally—through my body and nervous system—did something fundamental shift. For the first time in my life, I understood this: Safety does not come from outside you. It is generated within. And when safety lives inside you, power follows. Not aggressive or egoic power. Not performative power. But an unshakeable, grounded, almost fuck-you kind of power. True certainty lives within. Your body is not just protection. It is grounded power—available on demand.

Your Divine Instrument

Your body is a gift entrusted to you. I am deeply grateful for my body. I love my body fully and completely—every facet of it, including the ones I once rejected. Today, hate isn't a word I use in any category. I don't need it. When you live in forgiveness and peace, that word bears no weight.

Back to the body. You are responsible for fine-tuning it, caring for it, and listening to it. And allowing God to move through it—through you. You are a divine flow-through. As is everything you create. Your life's offering is your energetic signature—the unique way you walk out the mission you came here to live. And I don't know about you, but I'm on a mission: more life, more love, more generosity, more contribution, more shared experience. No two roles or souls are the same. Comparison is wasted energy—in every form. And, there's more than enough to go around—one person having does not equal someone else having not. There's a quote I've always loved, written on the chalkboard of my former spin studio years ago:

> "To give anything less than your best is to sacrifice the gift."—Steve Prefontaine.

Pay attention to what excites you—and act on it. That excitement exists for a reason. It's a clue in the 'right' direction. Follow the hunches, even when they don't make sense in the moment. Clarity often reveals itself over time, sometimes only in hindsight. This is why trust matters—trust in yourself, and trust in the process—without requiring proof in advance. Notice what and who magnetize you. Your body always knows. What gives you energy, what drains it. Ask God to use you—to make you effective, to make you useful. Then take the first step—and keep asking.

How the Body Speaks

Pain is a messenger. Illness is information. What is buried alive stays alive—until it is met, moved, and released. Unprocessed emotion doesn't disappear. Ignored long enough, it speaks through the body. Breakdown is often what happens when we refuse to listen. I've lived this. I experienced it in a long-term relationship—one I didn't want to end, because the love itself was real, even when parts of the dynamic were not healthy. Over time, that relationship transformed into forgiveness, perspective, and eventually a deeper, more dimensional friendship. But while I was staying—my body was signaling—more like screaming.

When toxicity—whether environmental or relational—is ignored, the body speaks to you through you: cystic acne, ulcers, hair loss, chronic inflammation, uncharacteristic personality and behavior. The symptoms vary, but the message is consistent. Your body will get your attention when your mind tries to rationalize what your heart already knows. The invitation is to listen early—before intensive repair is required. Some breakdowns are visible. Others are not. I've known people who have gotten throat cancer and died—after years of suppressing their truth. I've known people who carried guilt for things that were never theirs to hold, despite being vibrant, loving souls. This expressed as issues in the blood—and death as well. These stories aren't here to scare you. They're here to remind you of something simple and profound: Shame, guilt, anger, neglect—these energies need ushering along; dissolving, release. They need honesty. They need compassion. Left unaddressed, they settle into the body and take up residence—only to inevitably express in unhealthy, negative and sometimes catastrophic ways—sometimes too late to catch. Signals through the body that we get to acknowledge, face and heal or transform—are not punishment. They are guidance. The deeper blessing is learning to purify your heart as you go—to stay in truth, to course-correct early, to choose grace over self-abandonment. No one does this perfectly. I certainly didn't. We do not need to live and learn the hard way.

The Power of The Heart

At the core, every human wants the same thing: to love and be loved, to be seen and accepted, to belong. Yet much of the world is unconsciously addicted to pain—soothing instead of healing, avoiding instead of calmly confronting. Love and fear are the two governing forces. Every decision is rooted in one or the other. This single question changes everything: Does this expand me—or contract me? When I committed—unconsciously at first, then deliberately—to the purification of my heart, everything began to shift. The areas of my life that needed cleaning up started resolving themselves. Less friction. More calm. Greater clarity. Ease of deliverance to me for me—zero elements of chasing, forcing, controlling, manipulating or manufacturing. Honesty with the heart is pivotal and powerful. When you are honest about what your heart wants, life has more room to go right. When you deny yourself or override your truth, not only do you feel worse—life becomes heavier. Even the smallest actions require more effort. So how do you purify the heart? Begin by creating coherence—between brain and heart—and let the subconscious do what it already knows how to do. In that state, insight arrives. Rest deepens. Guidance becomes clearer. Healing unfolds. Life responds when you do. Willingness and courage are required.

Sleep and Dream-state

We'll return to sleep and dreams in their own chapter, but it's essential to name this here. Sleep is the ultimate repair. In deep sleep, the body cleanses, restores, and detoxifies—especially the brain. More on this in a future chapter.

My Younger Self's Mantra

This may sound simple—but it worked. In 2015, after elective bunion surgery (on both feet, for function—not vanity—though be aware I am Mrs. Vanity at the core), I was suddenly forced into stillness. I had always moved my body daily—being an athlete and dancer, and the abrupt inability to do so terrified me at first. Like a literal cutting off of a limb. A core daily activity for mental stability, joy—and the physical benefits. Then something shifted. In the quiet of recovery, a mantra arrived—unprompted, instinctive: "I am healthy and hot no matter what." It wasn't affirmation for the sake of positivity. It became a belief—and my body followed. That period taught me something unexpected: my sense of vitality wasn't dependent on constant physical output. Movement mattered, yes—but mindset mattered just as much. I trusted my body. I listened to my energy. I ate well. And I stayed connected to myself instead of fighting what was. The result? A body I had a deep appreciation for—true strength, greater ease. That mantra rewired my relationship with my body. No matter the shape or size, I was healthy and hot—because I decided so. And sometimes, the deciding is enough.

This Shape Shifts Physical Appearance

Love is the most powerful force in existence. It heals. It nourishes. And it reshapes the body—and the face. When I have felt safe, seen, and loved properly, stress, unworthiness and shame I didn't know I had have literally melted off my body and my face. My features softened. Eyes brightened. My posture changed—and I've always had good posture; I'm a dancer. My nervous system decompressed and exhaled. The body holds weight and inflammation as protection. This isn't failure or punishment—it's intelligence. When I was younger and obsessed with being ultra-lean, my mother once said, "Your body needs a little skin on your bones to protect you if you get sick." I took that to the bank. Meaning, I took that seriously. I stopped obsessing over being thin and chose to focus on strong. And real strength, I learned, requires softness—vulnerability, grace, and openness. Not armor or a caged heart. My heart's never been caged—I'm saying this for someone who maybe this is the case. I have never looked—or felt—better than when I was being loved properly. The inverse when not, I've looked and felt dull and decayed. Human connection is the most powerful drug on earth; it is the medicine. Let love rule.

Food and Energetic Layers

Every body requires different nourishment. Resist the urge to tell others what they need. Focus on yourself. At different points in time, your body and soul may ask for different forms of nourishment. This is the body in true intelligence communicated. I love food. I'm not a "foodie," but I deeply appreciate good cuisine. For me, less is more for a handful of reasons. There is a sweet spot between not enough and too much. That sweet spot is called satiation. I eat to support energy, mental clarity, and satiety—not heaviness. Notice how you feel when you're sluggish or zapped. That heaviness, to me, is a frequency sabotage. We are light bodies. Heavy inputs create density. Now notice how you feel when you meditate. When my body isn't weighed down by heavy food, I access a golden, expansive state and connection with the field with ease. When I'm overfed—or fed foods that don't support me—that access becomes muted and limited. Less light. More drag. Harder to reach higher states of awareness and super-consciousness. During my Yoga Nidra training, I learned about the yogic layers of the body—the kosha's. I've always thought of them not as layers, but as multi-bodies.

For reference, these are the bodies (layers):

- Annamaya Kosha (food sheath) is the physical body (skin and bones).

- Pranamaya Kosha (vital sheath) is the energy body (breath, etc.)
- Manomaya Kosha (mental sheath) is the mental-emotional body (thoughts and feelings).
- Vijnanamaya Kosha (wisdom sheath) is the discerning body (intellect and intuition processing).
- Anandamaya Kosha (bliss sheath) is the bliss body and the inner-most layer to the true self.

These bodies are interconnected. When one is imbalanced, the whole system feels it. Each layer has its own spectrum of lightness or density. When there is clarity, cleanliness, and ease—the body responds accordingly.

A Thing of Beauty

Mind, heart, energy—this is all beauty. And so is the body—so let's please not condemn the physical. We live in a world where visual beauty is a multibillion-dollar industry. Pretending otherwise doesn't make us enlightened—it just makes us dishonest. Let's look at beauty through a different lens: joy, ownership, creative agency and expression. Beauty isn't hair, makeup, clothes, or a specific body type. Beauty is feeling good in your own skin—however that is. Loving who you are. Allowing yourself to be creatively expressed—however that looks for you. I'm pro-procedure, whatever the choice, because I believe in agency. I believe in doing what feels aligned for you—without shame or justification. You owe no one an explanation.

I've heard people say makeup is disempowering. For others, it's art. For some, it's grounding. For some, they could not care less. All of that can be true at once. What makes it beautiful isn't the choice. It's the ownership. Different cultures relate to beauty differently. In France, I heard commentary on American makeup being "too much," paired with a deep reverence for natural elegance. In America, makeup is often part of self-expression—playful, bold, creative. Neither is right nor wrong. Climate even plays a role. In humid places—the Caribbean, Miami, the South of France—my skin glows effortlessly. Makeup feels optional. In drier, colder climates, a little help to add color and dimension back in feels like a breath of fresh air. Is it necessary? No. Is it fun? Absolutely. For me, makeup has always been a comfort ritual. Grounding. I remember being seventeen, having moved to a new city, knowing no one. Dance class. Work. That was my world. And then—wandering into a MAC Cosmetics counter, where a kind woman named Leanne opened my eyes to this fun world and taught me. I had a major blush obsession back then and still do. It wasn't about looking a certain way. It was about expression. How do I want to look today? How do I want to feel? What mode of the avatar am I putting on today? Choice, fun, identity—and change. Beauty is not about fitting into someone else's standard. What makes it beautiful isn't the choice, it's the ownership.

4

CHAPTER FOUR

GRACE AND ALLOWING

Release Control—and the Pressure

Take life seriously—with a light heart. Grace lives in being, not effort. People's language is revealing. What lives beneath spoken words isn't hard to hear—the challenge is listening. Awareness hides in plain sight, stitched quietly into daily moments that look ordinary until you really see them. Life is layered. We peel one layer back and another reveals itself. Mastery of self is often nothing more than the courage to keep peeling. I've had moments when the thesis I was proving turned out to be me. I've lived that more than once. Moments where something clicks and the quiet mystery you've been inhabiting suddenly reveals itself. Especially in the years after my head injury—through post-traumatic stress and then into the quieter revelation of what it means to live without anxiety or the need to control—I learned this: anxiety can dissolve. Trauma lodges itself into the body, and it has to be unwound and rewired there. How deeply it's lodged depends on the layers.

For years I believed I had surrendered—thirteen years ago, eight years ago, and again more recently. Only later did I see how filling every hour with being productive, achieving, and scheduling was its own subtle form of control. I believed space had to be filled. Grace, I learned, lives in the space itself. When this finally clicks, it lands with a lightness—but powerfully. Ironically, this simple truth took me longer to understand than problems I've solved with ease. No matter how evolved we think we are, each of us is always a beginner somewhere. To create space is to expand time. Presence isn't just showing up—it's softening into the moment until it opens. I've always lived motion. But even my rest was active. Grace doesn't come naturally to everyone. For those who once measured worth through achievement, it's a muscle—stretched, and trained. Recovery requires flexibility. A head injury demands stamina. So does returning to yourself. Strength is built in quiet repetitions until one day it feels effortless.

Grace extends beyond the self—to parents, loved ones, and those who came before us. I believe most people do the best they can with what they have until proven otherwise. Rather than living in resentment, I choose forgiveness, compassion, and forward motion. We don't remember events as they were—we remember them as we are. Forgiveness is power. It releases you from rehearsing the past. Grace often looks like courage: beginning again, reinvention, walking away from what once defined you. These aren't steps backward—they're leaps wrapped in small actions. Grace lets you hold the unknown without collapsing. Clarity follows. And clarity is power. My grace was forged through many things:

- Years of recovery—head injury, post traumatic stress, questioning my own sanity
- The courage to change careers, cities, relationships of all kinds
- A refusal to live a small or meaningless life

Life refines us so we can hold what we're meant to receive. During my recovery in 2018, I listened daily to Joel Olsteen. I still remember Joel's teddy bear story: if only we'd release the small one we cling to, we'd see the much bigger one waiting. Simple. True. Sometimes we cling to what's familiar because we can't yet imagine something better. Grace, at its essence, is loosening the grip—and trusting what remains.

5
CHAPTER FIVE
PEOPLE AND MIRRORS

Eras

I AM BLESSED beyond measure in this category. I will never forget those who were there for me when I needed everything they gave—a place to sleep, pajamas to wear, food to eat, presence, and things money cannot buy. There were times. And I've been that person too—opening my world when someone needed a safe place. The constant has been this: we were there for each other.

I begin here in gratitude—for the people in my world, past, present, and future. There are people I've met in dreams who later appeared in real life. It is our relationships—and the experiences we share through them —that give life its depth. My inner circle is tight. Sacred. Unwavering. Beyond it, the net of kindness, generosity, and inclusion spreads wide.

There's something special about the eras of our lives—what simply was. No force. No overthinking. Just truth, lived and loved out loud. Often on the dance floor. My high school friends—though we're no longer in regular contact (minus a few)—carry a silent, fierce loyalty. We may not speak often, but the bond remains. Clear. Unspoken. Certain.

Friends of my early twenties—the years of leaving home, post-secondary life, and the party era—left their imprints. Beautiful ones. Necessary ones. Lessons learned—and thankfully, not repeated. A handful remain close; the rest live on as memories or acquaintances. Some have been consciously released.

Then there are the friends met along the way—by reason, by season, by lifetime. The ones you meet on holiday. The ones beside you in a crowded place. The ones you bump into on the street, on airplanes, in moments that accelerate growth. For some of us, there is no Plan B. We go straight through—no matter what it takes.

Each one meaningful. Each one formative. Each reflecting something back to me I could not have accessed alone. We meet ourselves through others.

Let It Rip

Being yourself matters more than anything. Say the thing. Ask. Don't hold back. Looking back, many of the most defining moments in my life came from honesty—from speaking when it would have been easier to stay quiet. A photoshoot in 2017 that I rescheduled after a night that had me in tears led me to the makeup artist who connected me to my immigration lawyer. Without that night, that reschedule, and that openness, my life would look very different. Moving to Miami was the same. I knew almost nothing about the city—just that it had a beach, sunshine, and an international airport. I reached out to someone I knew, and one connection led to the next. A showing turned into a call, a call into a decision. I signed that day. Alignment rarely arrives in ways you can plan. It arrives through people—through moments—through willingness to be seen. Some people land on your heart, change you forever, and never truly leave—no matter the distance. Every encounter refines you. Let it.

Weight of Value

Relationships carry different weight. Cherish them all—but keep close those who light up your heart and soul. There's a reason you feel that. Relationships require energy—not effort in the exhausting sense, but care. Presence. Intention. Some friendships are soft and spacious. Some are vibrant and electric. Some exist across time and distance with nothing required beyond genuine regard. Others are built through years of showing up—through joy, fracture, repair, and growth. I'm drawn to people who are doing the work—who care about how they move through the world. Who they are becoming. And I notice when resonance fades. Not dramatically—just naturally. We are always choosing who we stand beside.

Who You Do Life With

I once outsourced my happiness. That power is yours.

There was a time I poured almost everything into one relationship. I had friends—but I wasn't tending them. Then my mother died—unexpectedly. My world shifted quickly. I saw how few relationships were truly beside me—and whether they were the ones that I wanted to move forward with. I made myself a promise that day: never again. I don't fill space with bodies to avoid being alone. I share my time with those I feel called toward. If there's no depth, I quietly disengage—not out of coldness, but clarity.

Today, I have aligned, soul-nourishing friendships because of a decision I made: I will be an exceptional friend—and I will grow alongside people. I respect. And I do. These are lifelong bonds. And there is always room for new ones.

Seeing Beyond Labels

Don't be blinded by degrees, titles, shiny objects (humans that you may have on a pedestal) or by credentials. My stepbrother never cared much for school—yet his frequency was magnetic. Never without a girlfriend growing up. Now married to the love of his life with a family the past almost 20 years. He read Shakespeare for pleasure. Learned Chinese out of love. Did not care about the opinion of others and had no desire to fit in. True power isn't obedience. Its presence. His life—built on devotion, truth, and love—reflects alignment, not labels. When the inside is right, the outside follows. Our bond has always been resonance, not proximity. He stood next to me while I read my mom's eulogy. Silent support means everything in a moment it counts. Ties that are strong don't require constant contact to remain in bond.

Background Dancers

Pay attention to the background dancers in your life—the ones working quietly behind the scenes, tending to subtle pieces of your world. The ones whose presence brings calm, ease, or quiet joy. My aunt, my mother's sister, used to call herself a backup dancer—present, involved, without needing to be center stage. What she understood instinctively is that many of the most impactful people are not the loudest ones. She showed me that life doesn't need to follow a prescribed timeline. That fulfillment doesn't require conformity. That owning your own timing is power. The neighbor who says hello. The grocer you see each week. The people you pass on walks. The small interactions that land exactly when you need them. The little things are the big things. Much of what allows us to shine is built by people who never ask for the spotlight.

Family

Family comes in many forms. It isn't defined by blood alone. Family are the ones who show up. Not for photos—for real moments. The ones who stand beside you when it matters. The ones who see you fully—and stay. It's not proximity. It's presence.

The Real Ones

True friends are often outliers—nonconformists, path-makers, quiet rebels. You recognize them instantly. No announcement required. Friends evolve. Some bonds deepen. Others dissolve. The strongest ones grow alongside you—not always in the same direction, but in resonance.

6
CHAPTER SIX
WEALTH

We are born self-sustaining. Self-healing. Self-generating. Power is either accessed—or left unused.

I saw this early, through my grandparents. I remember one of my grandmothers saying, "If I want something, I don't want to have to ask anyone for it." She took care in how she showed up—every day. A talented seamstress, she made things, fixed things, created her own way.

My grandfather was quieter—but the same. When he wanted something, he didn't hesitate. He decided—and followed through. These weren't grand acts. They were decisions. They were also wise—thoughtful about how money moved, so there was always enough—to host, to give, to live without tension.

That stayed with me.

Money is a lens through which we see—and a reflector through which we experience. My set point was healthy from the beginning—until it wasn't. Getting it back required more than effort. It required deep reprogramming.

Your Level of Expectancy

Long before I had language for it, I carried a quiet assumption: there would always be enough. We were lower middle class. Nothing extravagant. But my mother had a way of making ordinary life feel opulent. Each room in our home was thoughtfully decorated. She knew how to stretch a dollar and make it count. Needs were met. I never went without—although there were times I wished I had more. Back then, I was style-obsessed without being able to express it.

In my early twenties, I stepped into industries expanding rapidly—oil and gas, then private equity focused on the resource sector. Compensation was better than average. Performance-based. Growth was expected. I did the work. Results followed. Money moved easily. It wasn't even a thought aside from appreciating it.

In relationships, we traveled. Ordered what we wanted. Said yes without calculation. I didn't analyze any of it. I assumed continuity.

Then, somewhere in my mid-30s, my baseline cracked.

Mind Others' Projections of Their Noise

Rewinding. At twenty-two, I received my first serious offer. Strong base. Bonuses. Autonomy. My boss expected me to grow into the role—and told me to expect more. He laid the game out clearly. He was at the end, I was at the start.

When I told my mother, her response carried doubt. Not overt—but enough to shift something in me. What had been ease became effort. She came from a world where rewards arrived slowly, over time. My pace didn't fit her timeline.

I still believed in myself. But something subtle wobbled. Later, the pattern repeated at higher levels. Are you sure? Is that sustainable? How did that happen?

The questions weren't about me. They reflected inherited ceilings.

But when disbelief enters the room—even gently—it interrupts expectancy unless that foundation is already stable. At the time, it was unconscious. Once I became aware of it, I began to over-analyze.

Internal Codes

For most of my life, money arrived easily—until it didn't. Nothing about my capability changed. I was still disciplined. Still showing up.

What shifted was internal.

At one point, I chose to step away from a career I had once been fully engaged in—and into a relationship where I became the supporting role. It wasn't forced. I chose it. And for a time, it worked—until it didn't. The structure of that life didn't support both—a big career and the role I had taken on. Something had to give.

Over time, something in me did.

A narrative repeated—quietly, consistently—that what I was doing wasn't enough, that I needed to do more, be more. And eventually, I began to question myself.

That was the shift.

After, something felt amnesic—like I had lost access to my own baseline. I started tracking everything, measuring contribution, staying in motion to justify my place.

Looking back, I can see where I outsourced my power—without realizing it at the time. It reduced everything to what actually mattered.

The rebuild that followed required returning to myself—steadily, deliberately, and with full conviction. Clarity returned—and there was no turning back. Not as something new, but as something that had always been there.

Standards and Core Stability

Growing up, I had ambitions. I wanted to build something of my own—to create, to operate, to move independently. At the same time, there was a quieter narrative present—one that leaned toward being looked after. Both existed, and what isn't consciously chosen tends to take the lead.

Then came a period that stripped everything down. The loss of my mother. The aftermath of outsourcing my power. A head injury that disrupted my ability to function the way I once had—all within a short window. What remained was simple: me. Stability became non-negotiable.

The rebuild wasn't glamorous, but it was real—and chosen. Internal steadiness had always mattered. I just hadn't protected it. Now, it's the rhythm I operate from. Chaos, especially when disguised as opportunity, has no appeal. Emotional volatility isn't worth the trade.

Money began returning the way truth does—quietly and consistently once I became steady enough to hold it. Internally set. Belief is contagious.

Allergic to Insecurity

"Allergic to insecurity" is a phrase someone I deeply appreciate says. It applies to everything—but especially to money. Who is drawn to insecurity? No one. Certainty magnetizes. I know how I move when I feel financially secure—even without guarantees. There's steadiness. My decisions are clean and clear. There's no underlying urgency, no tension driving my behavior. I'm not carrying or projecting worry.

The people I've learned from and admired most carry themselves the same way. Even when things are uncertain—no undertone of fear. Just an anchored, unwavering stance. Internal set points are real. The external rarely leads—it reflects.

Generational Shifts and Conscious Wealth

I admire how younger generations approach money—with less inherited weight and more expectancy. When money isn't tied to guilt or over-explanation, it moves more freely.

At a certain point, I stopped justifying my wants, my needs, or my worth. Justification isn't required when something is already inherent. Money creates options, movement, speed, relief, and comfort. It remains neutral.

7
CHAPTER SEVEN
CAREER AND CONTRIBUTION

Instinct Without Attachment

Doing what comes naturally is real. Most of what I'm genuinely good at comes from instinct. A quiet attunement—sometimes conscious, sometimes not. It's the only way I can explain how I moved through wealth management, and how I've navigated any creative endeavor. I've known. Not haphazardly. Not impulsively. Just instinctively—as a remembrance from the inside out. The finished product is never magic. It's the result of a million small decisions—each one taken in sequence consistently. At the core of it is self-trust without over-analysis. This is the difference between listening inward and being governed by external logic alone.

What Is It Really

What has served me well is giving breathing room—not quitting. More is not always more. In all things, there is a point of diminishing returns. I return to principle before checking boxes for my ego. Right and wrong are rarely universal here—perception shapes outcome. I find myself in a quiet conundrum because I love a multitude of projects. They are expressions of the heart. The real discernment lies in knowing what is heart-led—and what is ego-driven. The soul comes here to expand and evolve, but expansion is not synonymous with constant doing. Sometimes growth is found in being. This is where discernment matters. Some missions require sustained focus. Others require completion—and a redirection of energy altogether. When contribution is honest and sufficient, legacy takes care of itself. Relevance does not require constant visibility—although omnipresence is real, and is a valid tactic of many. The ripple of your energy moves whether you are seen or not. Before judgment, understanding. Not every calling is public. Some are quiet. Gifts differ.

What I've Learned

There are no right or wrong answers here. What follows is simply my lived perspective—through experience, hindsight, and foresight. Living in France and on the island, I noticed people didn't lead with what they did for work. Conversation didn't begin with titles, income, or neighborhoods. In North America, more weight is often placed on how someone makes money, as if a role carries moral value or determines worth. This is an observation, not a judgment. We are a sum total—and no one part needs to define us unless we allow it. Over time, I moved away from the word purpose and toward the word meaning. Purpose can feel heavy—something to hunt down or prove. Meaning feels lighter. It's not about the role itself, but the quality of energy you bring to everything—every person, role, interaction, contribution. Energy determines outcomes. Excellence isn't reserved for prestigious positions—it's a way of being. I've always admired people who show up in excellence. Once, while staying at The Carlyle in New York City, a doorman left a deeper impression on me than many individuals in 'higher' regarded roles I've met. He wasn't trying to impress. He was present, grounded, fully himself—in his authority. That impression stayed with me. Energy and truth over everything.

Respect for All and Identifying As

I've also encountered professionals with every credential imaginable—elite degrees, polished résumés, rehearsed confidence—whose presence felt hollow. No depth. No discernment. Credentials without coherence do not land. I respect higher education deeply—but without embodiment and application, it means little. Roles differ. Humanity doesn't. Time also doesn't determine the quality of experience someone has. Some people are talents out of the gate—that time could never. Time refines, and it's not always required to have anyone be at the level. Years ago, during a personal development training, we weren't allowed to discuss our professions. At first it felt strange—then freeing. Without career identifiers to lean on, everyone had to show up as human first, résumé second. It revealed something important: when identity is overly tied to what you do, disruption can feel like collapse. Pride is healthy. Attachment is not. I've lived that.

When I exited financial services full time, my ego took

a hit. It was an identity shift I hadn't prepared myself for. I was accustomed to external validation—daily reinforcement that I was capable, competent, exceptional. Replacing that dopamine took time. Then it dissolved. External validation becomes unnecessary when you're solid within yourself. Years prior, the moment that changed my life wasn't a promotion. It was "fired". The first person of what would become a massive round of layoffs. I was twenty-three. Performing well. Delivering results. And then it was over—decided by people who didn't know me, didn't understand my value, and wouldn't feel the fallout. My direct boss—the one who hired me, trained me, believed in me—was excluded from the decision. He found me afterward, visibly angry in the way only a grounded leader can be. He said, "This is a good thing. You have a head start on what's better than this." He wasn't consoling me. He was telling the truth. That moment showed me healthy leadership for the first time—encouraging, emotionally regulated, non-micromanaging. He pushed me forward, never down. I'm deeply grateful for him and the ripple that followed.

It also revealed something I couldn't unsee: if someone else can alter your entire trajectory with one decision, your life is not fully yours. To me, that's anxiety. Not because corporations are inherently untrustworthy—but because dependency at that level was no longer going to be acceptable as a way of life for me.

Years later, I saw the same pattern in boutique wealth management. Visionary firms—full of talent and humanity—would be acquired, and freedom would shrink. Compliance began working against not with. Expansion became contraction. It felt like watching a sparkler fizzle out, a curtain drop, and the piano stop playing. I believe in structure. I value systems and order. But leadership matters. Vision sets direction. Values shape culture. Energy is the environment. When those shift, what once felt expansive becomes a cage. For some, that feels safe. For me, it felt asphyxiating. My resistance was never to rules—it was to misalignment. To environments that required shrinking or 'molding' to belong. Once you see that disconnect, you can't unsee it. That's the point where what once worked stops yielding the same result. Leaving wasn't rebellion. It was a state of savior—for my integrity, my health, my soul. Redirection comes. Resistance it only prolongs the inevitable.

When Change Is Required

Six weeks before finishing this manuscript, I said out loud, "Reveal anything standing in my way." Everything surfaced at once—not as punishment, but as clarity. What returned was simple—and a come-to realization one morning when I was doing my stretches and movement. More is sometimes not more. The simple thing is often the potent thing. Those we are serving don't need "more". They need right.

My concussion taught me this. Burnout taught me this. Life kept reinforcing the same truth: less, done extremely well, moves mountains. Who you are behind closed doors is the real credential. Emotion is information to evaluate. I learned this in trading. Markets move on emotion; good decisions do not. Early discipline served me well, but also made me naïve. I took people at their word. Sometimes that's a gift. Sometimes it burns. Stillness reveals what busyness hides. Why do you think some people keep themselves "busy"? It's unconsciously strategic—avoidance, protection. The truth eventually surfaces.

When the noise fell away, I met myself. That became the real work. This book was assigned. I didn't dream it up. I reluctantly accepted a call. Everything is an invitation—we choose whether to answer. I've failed, pivoted, reinvented, rebuilt. Your career is not your identity. Your title is not your essence. How you move through the world matters most.

Stretching Forward

At this stage of my life, I choose intentional stretch—without unnecessary stress. I love to work because I love creating—I love a catalytic project and working with others—something that evokes emotion and moves people into motion. Life in motion is a beautiful thing. Earlier criteria were simple:

- I'm good at it
- Mutual exchange exists
- I enjoy delivering quality

Now, I listen for subtler, but much more clear nudges—projects that arrive with excitement, ease and alignment. These aren't forced. Strategy can be copied, alignment and the flow through of God-given gifts, can't. Stretching requires becoming someone new—another layer of you. Sometimes fear is the cost of admission. Do it anyway.

8

CHAPTER EIGHT

SAFE TO BE SEEN

Unshakeable

Safety isn't only a state in the body-mind—it's something we learn to perform. We learn it when our best is never enough. When love feels conditional. When acceptance wavers instead of holds. So we adapt. We soften our edges and temper our being. We walk on eggshells instead of being who we really are. True safety is a return to yourself. When it lands, something unshakeable settles in. It feels like an exhale. Drama no longer sticks. Chaos loses access. You recalibrate to a calm, steady power source—your Self.

Safety in the Body

When you feel safe in your body, life looks different. Safety changes how you move. You stop negotiating your existence. You step into rooms you once would have avoided. Growth has a cost. I have placed myself in acutely uncomfortable situations repeatedly since twenty-two—and accelerated that process at thirty-five. Time doesn't matter. Age doesn't matter. Friends, lovers, strangers—even fleeting encounters—are all mirrors reflecting you back to yourself. The mirror can't reflect what isn't present. You have to first appear.

When Safety Shatters

For me, this understanding was tested in my own body. Something I never knew was possible—until the feeling of it's anchor completely vanished. For many people, the sense of safety—or lack of it—in being seen exists deep within. For others, it's a daily act of courage. I became acutely aware of this after my accident—the one that left me with long-term post-concussion symptoms, phantom pain moving like static through my body, and post-traumatic stress anchored deep in every fiber of my being. It stripped away my voice. My ability to articulate coherent thought. Before that, I had never questioned safety in my body, my visibility, or my presence in the world. After, it became everything.

Feeling unsafe to be seen.

Stripped of my voice.

Unsafe even within my own skin.

That became the temporary norm.

Being seen was no longer about acceptance. It became a mission of reclamation—learning to feel safe enough to show up again—and do life. Post-traumatic stress and concussion can create profound unsafeness in the body—a resistance to visibility. Fortunately safety can be relearned.

CHAPTER 8

A Hollywood Treasure

A Saturday night in June, 2022. I called ahead to say our party would be late. Voicemail: "Due to unforeseen circumstances, Mr. Chow's will be closed for the evening." That was that.

Fast-forward to Javier's in Century City. A mall for dinner on a Saturday night? I was skeptical—but the night was better than one I'd imagine. Every turn led us there—even a pit stop at Shake Shack of which a can of white wine followed us into Javiers. A packed restaurant—front room. A back room with only standing space. Three guys at the bar—the kind you could've gone to high school with—waved us over to "share their bartender." Conversation sparked effortlessly and immediately deepened—while still remaining light in heart. At that time, I felt like a shell of myself—not my best version. I felt socially awkward—unlike me. I'm a natural social butterfly once I'm out. But this was different. Living in fight-flight still years after my accident. Feeling unsafe in my body and still learning to feel safe being seen. Two of them stood directly in front of me—grounded and fully present. Not intimidating in the least bit. We talked about Canada. We talked about LA. About love. About why we all felt strangely at home in that city. It was their hometown and was my city for 2 years at one point. This time I was a visitor. I mentioned I was staying at the Beverly Wilshire. One smiled. "He grew up a few blocks from there." I asked why they were out for the night and they mentioned it was sort of a bachelor party. When I asked about the wedding and where it would be held, they sighed. San Diego. She's from there. Doesn't like LA. A collective rolling of eyes. Then something shifted. Real talk replaced small talk. "What do you love most about her?" I asked. He smiled. "She's just a good person." Intuitively I knew that was not his person, but I never said anything. Later I found out that wedding never happened. The other spoke about fatherhood. We came up with a plan for him to start taking his daughter on daddy-daughter dates. Loves his wife. Great, longtime relationship and marriage. Two of us shared about our love for surf. I said, "It feels like we've known each other since high school—just older, better looking, and wiser." They smiled and agreed. They offered margaritas. Food. Anything. I wanted nothing but water. Earlier that day I was at Wally's and had one too many rosé and Paloma—and at a time I rarely consumed alcohol; the afternoon cocktails, lunch and a disco nap at the hotel pool winded me. That was my tempo that night—simple, calm, straightforward—as always. When they invited us to join them at the next spot—the strippers, I smiled. "Thanks but no—that's not in my destiny tonight." The response was immediate: "You're rad as fuck." We hugged and parted ways.

Minutes later, walking through the warm night air, I realized who I had been talking to for hours. An actor and creative, whom everybody knows—and who has a heart of gold. I didn't even realize who he was in that moment. It was just one of those moments you wish suspended a little longer. A snapshot in time. Safe people exist and you feel them immediately. They meet you in truth and effortlessly invite you in. Some people carry calm because they fought for it themselves. When you let yourself be seen, the world and those meant for you meet you.

9

CHAPTER NINE

THE MIRAGE OF OPINION

Let Things Roll Off

LET THINGS TAKE THEIR COURSE. Stay in your lane. Focus on your own movie. There's a particular kind of freedom that arrives when you stop caring what others think—not because you're trying not to care, but because the thought simply stops crossing your mind. We each exist within our own constructs, paradigms, and frequencies. Harmony isn't about sameness; it's the quiet coexistence of differences—the acceptance that multiple truths can exist at once. That realization shifted something in me. For people in my outer orbit—some closer than others—who were never meant to be main characters in my story, I once tried to understand their unkindness. Often it comes from fear, insecurity, or simple self-absorption. Sometimes people are so absorbed in their own movie that you barely register. Meanwhile, you show up with kindness because that's who you are—not because you need acknowledgment. And that's enough. When that clicked, I stopped striving to be liked by most. I stopped editing myself to make others comfortable. I simply leaned into being myself—and existing with neutrality—in those 'rougher terrain' environments. I.e. people committed to making you wrong, overlooking you, etc, etc, etc. When a negative charge arises—from a person, a moment, or even my own reflection—I pause and ask: What is this really about? What am I meant to see, learn, release, or carry forward? Polarity is part of nature. Sometimes it's the stark contrasts that create the brightest light after a storm.

Different Parallels

One day you may find yourself living in an entirely new parallel—lighter, freer—on a train that no longer stops where it once did. That's called moving forward. Not everyone will be on board. Not everyone is meant to be. Bless people. Wish them well. And keep going. What you focus on expands. It took me too long to understand how powerful focus is. What you forgive and release gets to stay behind. Your space—now and ahead—is sacred. Energy is power. Power is choosing how, where, and with whom you spend it. Forward motion isn't a single decision. It's a quiet one you make again and again. When it comes to the past, my approach is simple: I rarely visit it. A fond memory here or there is welcome—like a flash of nostalgia. But what was forgettable never had staying power to begin with. What was painful has been processed and released. Old noise doesn't get to live rent free where peace and possibility reside. Sometimes someone from the past reaches out with sudden curiosity—someone you were never particularly close to. Years ago, that might have put me on guard. Today I see it differently. It isn't always malicious. Sometimes it's simply human nature. Sometimes it's proof that our lives ripple further than we realize. Integrity travels further than we think. While I've blown up and rebuilt various parts of my life, I'm not interested in burning bridges. If a parting of the ways is necessary, I simply allow the distance.

Pour Into Your Life

Become so immersed in improving your life, expanding your world, and pouring into what matters that the unimportant fades into the background like static on an old radio. There is a strange irony in writing people into and out of your script—because yes, the script is real. Roles you once longed to play may become roles you wouldn't accept today. Not because anyone is above anyone else. We are all equal. But we change. Standards change. Clarity changes. Vision changes. Sometimes your soul simply moves to a place that feels better. That is the quiet miracle of growth—rising out of invisible chains you didn't even know you were wearing. The air is clearer here. Like ocean air. It lives in the spaces—and with the people—who let you be exactly who you are. The ones who see you, love you, and allow you to remain yourself. You are the main character. Everyone else is supporting cast. No performance required.

PART III: ATTUNE

FINE TUNE

1

CHAPTER ONE

ST. BARTS AND THE FRENCH RIVIERA

THIS CHAPTER ISN'T about the location itself. Like many places and eras, it is a time capsule. Some snapshots last decades. Some are complete in the blink of an eye. After the last hurricane—and with easier access, less privacy, expanded development, and a shifting commercial landscape on a global scale—the energy changed quite dramatically.

When the Future Collapses Into the Present

This chapter of life felt like a postcard from a realm I had lived vividly in my mind long before I stepped onto that timeline in the physical. The experience was a series of improbable alignments—everything arriving just when it needed to. Not loud or dramatic, but precise. The last time I visited the island before moving there, I was observing without realizing it. My senses were wide open. Something inside me sparked—and pulled. The warmth on my skin. The dust of the winding roads. The nighttime breeze moving through palms, the stars, the small-town rhythm. It felt familiar. Not like creation—but recollection. As though some part of me remembered before I consciously did. The people, the place—even the famously complex French administration—became catalysts for expansion. Lessons I hadn't anticipated, but clearly required. A God-given vision is what led me to become a St. Barth resident in the fall of 2023. After a trip that April—a place I'd visited consistently for twelve years—I returned to my home in Vancouver (Canada), and immediately began researching how to live there long term. The very day I sent an email, it landed in exactly the right hands. Six months later, I was there on the ground. Creating a life. Rolling into Monoprix Home over Thanksgiving weekend, piecing together what would become home for the next undetermined stretch—which turned into just over a year.

That moment marked a recalibration. I was emerging from my head injury with a renewed sense of self. Fundamentally the same person—but clearer. After years of short-term memory disruption and waking to a slightly altered reality each day, clarity felt like oxygen. During my recovery, nothing that should have "made sense" was sticking. I understand now. The Caribbean carried ambiguity in some senses, and safety in others. Calm and simplicity—within administrative complexity.

The parts I loved about the island the most: genuine kindness and unconditional love appeared when I least expected them. They showed up in early mornings on the beach, evenings under the stars, simple moments, shared meals with people who made me feel like I belonged. Brief rendezvous encounters. Soul recognition at first site. Some routines I wish I could repeat forever—morning and afternoon hikes, morning surf sessions—and more time spent with people who feel like sunshine on the heart. Seeing people for face value was a thing here because not everyone was who they said they were. Why some people conceal their identity? I don't know. Maybe they want to be someone else but are stuck. I loved my island routine. If I could bottle it, I would. Choosing between the efficiency and scale of America and the privacy and presence of the island was not simple.

The Unexpected Detour to France

After eight months on the island, French administration being French administration, I had to relocate to mainland France to finalize my carte de séjour. Timing became divine. A friend was also spending the summer in the South of France. I released my property in St. Barths—choosing to surrender—and packed my life into five suitcases.

There is no buying two seats on AirFrance to travel with two dogs, so I needed a seat mate. In the SBH airport sitting in front of the angel flight booking agent, three calls were made. The last person said yes. A kind 25-year-old island ship captain became my travel companion for the twenty-some hours ahead. He was on the way home for the summer and to meet up with his family and girlfriend. Traveling to Nice with me was a slight detour for him, but he miraculously said yes. At Charles de Gaulle, we were exhausted. He got flagged at security for carrying a large amount of cash. Meanwhile, I had forgotten to check my cabin-sized Rimowa in St. Barths—too tired and emotional in the moment, meaning every full-size liquid I owned was in my carry-on. I prayed a Hail Mary as it went through the scanner—made eye contact with the girl who was security checking everything, looked at her with "Dear God please-eyes" and somehow, they cleared it. Thirty pounds of expensive liquids. Ladies, you get it. A miracle. I had to share this memory because it makes me laugh to this day. Not only that, we were about to miss our connection from Paris to Nice. In this moment we were grateful for a slight delay.

Leaving the island devastated me. Forward motion was required. That friendship continued—steady, supportive, uncomplicated. His French was better than mine, my English better than his, and yet we connected meaningfully.

Raised Standards

Some connections arrive like déjà vu. Some drop in to reawaken dormant parts of you or raise your standards. This friend was one of them—the runner I passed many mornings and evenings on one of the few roads that people run or walk. At the start of the season we passed each other all the time. Months passed. Then one morning we nearly collided. I took off my sunglasses and a silent captivation was shared. We were both stunned. You're still here? We finally stopped and spoke. And life rearranged itself instantly—as it does when it's meant to. We met for iced coffee that morning. Milk and sugar. Easy connection—joyful, childlike, curious. Minutes after parting, he texted: "I changed my flight. I'm staying a few more days in case I get the chance to see you!"

My response: "Yes of course!"

In him, I saw qualities I adore in myself: playfulness, strength, conviction, discipline, loyalty, vulnerability, presence, kindness, peacefulness, and vision. At the time, we were medicine for each other. The kind that arrives exactly when a lesson is ready to surface. Later, we found ourselves in the South of France at the same time—not together, but on the ground doing our own things.

When I landed, he called: "What do you need? If you don't tell me, I'll bring everything." And he did. Groceries, treats, facial sheet masks, chocolate, Nespresso pods, quiche, eggs, bread sticks, olive tapenade, fruit, chips, Haribo—kindness and care in motion. A summer of friendship with plans as we shared a locale was the intent, which—ended up being anything but.

Availability didn't match. Life happens. Patterns surfaced. The familiar one: accepting what was left over after everything else came first—or when plans changed or re-scheduled in an instant—this was all too similar to my childhood. At first it seems slight and micro, then it snowballs into something larger, buried deep within the subconscious. The change in plans to how I spent my time really was a blessing. I met the people I was meant to and grew as a person—that if I'd been in constant companionship, I would have never tapped into and uncovered what I needed to during that time. The upside: given the space that once would have been occupied—different angels on my path appeared instantly.

In our friendship at that time, there were absolutely golden moments: ice cream on the pier in Saint-Tropez or strolling around a nearby village, late dinner melting in the heat, laughter sharing tarte flambée, riding his motorcycle in the warmth with cicadas chirping through Collobrières, late afternoon Sundays on the beach, sun-soaked, into the perfectly crisp water, unbothered. Fleeting moments. Inside jokes. Kind, generous, not without flaws. Perfect as they are. Mutuality in seeing and accepting. True friendship. A breath of fresh air.

Calibration

Some people enter your life as reminders. Others as mirrors. A rare few arrive like a code you didn't know you'd been waiting to unlock. Kika was that. By the time I reached the South of France, I was ungrounded in ways I hadn't anticipated. Nine months on a protected island had rearranged my nervous system. Being launched back into the wider world felt abrupt. I didn't know how long I'd be there. I felt suspended — between countries, between chapters, between versions of myself. It wasn't logistics that shook me. I can survive anything. It was a contrast. There were people who had known me for years and still couldn't see me. Not fully. Not accurately. And then there was her —someone who barely knew me, yet met me without hesitation.

She didn't analyze me.

She didn't manage me.

She just accepted me.

There was an ease between us that felt structural, not emotional. Like two frequencies clicking into place. The realization hit me in the moment all at once. Not a tear. An internal river. The kind that surges through the body before the mind can comprehend. It wasn't about her. It was about the moment I understood that someone who had known me for weeks could see me more clearly than people who had known me deeper. That recognition cracked something open. I saw, in a flash, how long I had tolerated partial visibility. How often I had edited myself to maintain comfort for others. She didn't love me because she understood my history. She loved me because she recognized me. There is a difference. Her presence didn't build me. It revealed me. And in that revelation, something stopped asking to be chosen.

Countless Angels

My time between France and St. Barths was filled with extraordinary people. In St. Tropez, the villa concierge team protected and guided me in multiple moments. They were kind beyond measure. Their mistake with the keys led me to one of the most magical women I've ever met—who unlocked codes inside me I didn't know existed. A dying phone battery after walking around St Tropez one Sunday after misplacing my car led me into that very concierge office. Another angel, the photographer who took my séjour photo invited me to shoot for a coffee-table book, The Dogs of St. Tropez. That meeting led to kismet connections with her Dutch friends, conversations about love and life at Café des Arts. The most incredible facials, Marine. Each of these people entered my life by circumstance but stayed through resonance. These relationships remain meaningful because they were clear. Mutual. Real. I remain grateful for this snapshot in time—for the clarity it brought and the truth it confirmed. Maybe heaven on earth is simply this: a handful of people who see you, a place that unlocks something essential, and the knowing that—for a brief, luminous stretch—you were exactly where you were meant to be. The contrast wasn't external. It was internal. Joy and grief. Clarity and confusion. Beauty and pain. So you keep going. Back to the island I would return for a few more months—before the next choice arrived. Stay, or go. And that decision would come when it was ready.

2
CHAPTER TWO
AMERICA

Topanga Harvest Moon

THIS MORNING, nostalgia drifted into my awareness as I sipped my coffee. A particular aroma carried me back to Los Angeles—the end of summer 2018, about six months after the accident that shook me to my core. At the time, my home was on St. Johnswood Drive, near the Topanga Canyon Outlook. I love that pocket of the city—especially the massive dog park tucked into the base of the Santa Monica Mountains. That house was a kind of vortex. Its owner—also my friend—had created it with intention. She was moving through a divorce and living in a larger home; I needed a place. The exchange was mutual, simple, timely and perfect. I will treasure that pocket of time forever. We had another roommate, who was a balanced complement to the household. After the accident I'd lost my license for 18 months—having been given a distracted driving ticket. Anytime a ride was generously offered some place, I was in. We did Orange

Theory together. Bristol Farms. Mexican. The dog park. The most raw, honest, judgement-free conversations were had. The whole household, plus others we'd invite, celebrated high holidays together—despite many of us technically not being Jewish. That didn't matter. It was the desire and decision to share that time—and the assigned meaning. The whole of it had a sacred lightness when everyone was together. It was special. I will never forget the afternoon of Rosh we rolled into Venice and did a kundalini class at my friend's Rabbi's—led by the Rabbi. Everyone looked strangely healthy for their age—a great thing. The Rabbi's baby was there—and so chill the entire time. Good energy all around. Connective. Sacred. Pure. On the way home we stopped on the side of the PCH to toss bread into the ocean as part of that day's ritual.

While that season of my life felt like rock bottom in many ways, it was also woven with beauty and magic. I walked the canyon daily into Woodland Hills—always with my ride or die, Sadie, in tow. The dusty road, the morning light shimmering across the trees, the peaceful pace of putting one foot in front of the other became medicine. Those walks were stabilizing. They signified forward motion, deliberately, day after day. A subtle kind of consistency felt in my bones. Something to rely on. Something to look forward to. One early Saturday morning, I stopped at Starbucks. My card app or the Wi-Fi wasn't working. The only other person in the coffee shop, at 6am on a Saturday morning, noticed and stepped in, offering to pay just as my transaction finally went through. Still standing there, he asked, "What did you order?" "Liquid diabetes," I said without hesitation. That day, it was a peppermint white mocha—a rare indulgence even then. Today, that amount of sugar would probably tranquilize me. One thing led to another, and within minutes we were deep in conversation—vulnerability right out of the gate, mutual recognition. We stared at each other for a few minutes in silence before anything was said—like recognizing another from the very planet you come from. Curious why the Universe placed us where it did for that moment. He had green eyes, sandy hair, a chiseled face, and sun-kissed skin. Calm energy. Non-performative. Confident with nothing to prove. Direct. He was visiting his sister and her family for the weekend—in town with his 3 daughters, one checking out a college for the following year. Married young, grown children, divorced after healing into a healthier identity. People change, and life goes on—for those who want to keep living. Fleeting. Meaningful. For a handful of days, we shared small joys and connected with a childlike innocence that was food for the soul. Some people pass through like a fallen star. Brief, bright, reflecting, only reminiscent of one encounter. Leaving the reminder that you belong.

There were countless moments like that during that time—brief, human, unforgettable. Every person I encountered in real life during that chapter felt like medicine in some way. Through depth, joy and calm. Through humor and presence. Through simple, perfectly timed recognition. Those doing the work recognize one another. Life arranges meetings like that. God speaks through others straight to us—when we are open. You can feel when someone is a safe space. I'm grateful I got to be that for others—and that I was met by it in return. Even while everything around me felt unsettled, I was profoundly grateful. It was during this era that I learned how to create safety within myself. For the first two years after my accident, I had no fixed address. I rented rooms, lived without consistency, moved often. What looked unstable became formative. Flexibility became steadiness. My body, heart, and mind became the only home I could rely on. Safety isn't seasonal. Safe people are rare. I don't take them lightly. Looking back, I see that time for what it truly was: a liminal chapter filled with grace. A period where life stripped me down to the essentials and quietly taught me what actually matters. It's who we are being—and the company we keep—that shapes everything.

A Bit More Memory Lane

2019. My second space in LA was at the base of the Palisades on the PCH across the street from the ocean—close to Temescal Canyon—a place I'd walk up daily. My uniform at the time: leggings (they were strangely gorgeous, perfect seams—wow material), a white tank top—beater style, white Saint Laurent sneakers with leopard laces, my Panerai, Goyard and of course Sadie, my furry angel. I've always considered my hair part of the outfit. It's never been remarkable. It's the way we wear it that makes it.

While I looked like I could fit in—I was holding myself together by threads, quite literally. Speaking of textiles, I met the most kind woman at an upscale second hand shop in Palisades. The name of the store was Get Dressed, and the woman's name is Molly—I adore her. While I couldn't afford the goods at the time, I still window shopped in her store and she always treated me with kindness and dignity. All I wanted at the time was these cozy Sablyn cashmere sweaters. The common theme in my life: comfort and warmth. Anyway. I'll never forget her kindness. I will also keep the memories of mornings sitting outside of Sweet

Laurel—cake for breakfast, and still shopping at Erewhon despite living on the smallest grocery budget I've ever had in my life. Prior to moving to the Caribbean, I had a dream to move back to this location—Palisades Bowl. To buy an AirStream and if lucky, own the lease to a rarely available slice of land in the beachside mobile home park. I envisioned this home base—even if I eventually had another home in LA or some other place in the world. It was a dream to have a beach house. God redirected me—if even temporarily. LA has a way of making you feel like you belong—when you're honest about who you are. It weeds out people who aren't real. For me, I've only had good experiences and memories there and I am grateful. This could be my amnesia in primarily remembering the good, but—in this case, I'll take it.

Default Into Divine Doorway

When I left the Caribbean, Miami was the default. Similar climate. A hop skip and a jump. This scenario ticked the initial boxes. Quite literally a decision that took 5 minutes. But nothing about it was accidental. America was never a fallback. It was an in-my-bones decision made long before I knew how it would unfold. A certainty I carried as a child, without language or timeline attached. I didn't know how it would happen. I still don't know where it leads. I simply kept living—working, learning, taking the next step. Over time, those choices accumulated. Doors opened. Paths formed. What once felt distant became inevitable.

Home, I've learned, is a feeling—not a place. You know it the moment it arrives. I landed in Miami the Friday before Christmas. Exhausted. Relieved. My dogs and I went straight from the airport to a home we'd never seen in person. Two suitcases. Five boxes still en route. Nothing else. A home. One spot. On American soil. The space was completely empty—not a fork, not a hanger, not a pillow. So naturally, it being 7 p.m., we went to Target. Walking into those bright aisles, I whispered internally, A-fucking-men. All elements combined in that moment—it felt like home. Building a life after a head injury requires unrelenting grit. It took nearly a year before that space felt fully supportive. Each day was spent in appreciation—especially because I knew what it meant not to have a stable home. And a space where I was safe from other's casting their needs upon me before I could look after my own. Opportunity met preparedness. That's how it works. Decisions made with conviction lock things in. I ran toward this chapter with a full-body yes—and was prepared to do whatever it took. I did. I have. I continue to.

The Deepest Exhale

Those who know—know. Getting to do life and business in America is a blessing. And for me, the deepest exhale of my life. As a child, I crossed state after state with my father in his semi truck—each place its own world filled with history and nostalgia I'd once transported myself into through films—now real life. America felt vast, generous, alive with possibility. Even then, it felt like home. Every morning I wake here, I thank God. Every time I unlock my own door and step through the threshold, that feeling floods me again. I don't take it for granted. For anyone who has left one world to begin another, you understand. In this country, willingness matters. Home of the Brave and the free is accurate.

There is no running away nor abandonment for those of us who have chosen to live dreams outside where we were born. It's merely an adventure and a calling of the soul that cannot be denied. The place where you can finally exhale—where life feels resonant, grounded, and aligned—is home. Maybe it's not even a location, it's you, in your body—and those you are with. It's a feeling, not a place. But in this case, it's also a place. And I chose it.

As an Immigrant and Learning from Them

Whether to a neighboring country or across the world—if you are one, you know the feeling. The dream. The belonging. My immigration experiences have taken me from Canada to the Caribbean, France, and to America. Everyone makes their choices for different reasons—and all are valid. I have a deep respect for those who follow that call.

Living in Vancouver was my first real window into this. So many immigrants. So many hardworking people bringing their vision to life—uniquely and beautifully. And yet, I often witnessed them not being given full respect. It broke my heart—and at times had me in fury; I am a protector and a stand for equality. But what struck me more was this: most of them didn't flinch. Like, not 2 fucks given. They knew who they were. Take it or leave it. They didn't let outside judgment shake them. They had a vision. They were focused on what mattered—family, the people they were supporting, the life they were building. I learned a lot about unshakeable self-worth from them—and what humble power really looks like.

My Vietnamese landscaper—and his team he cared and provided opportunities for.

My Hungarian fashion designer.

My Persian kickboxing coach.

Each are part of my soul family.

To name a few.

I love them—and many others. So much respect.

I carry an element of their essence with me as I bring my own dreams to life. This is simply a thank you.

We are all visitors here. Stewards, wherever we are.

And wherever we are—

be all there.

3
CHAPTER THREE
INNER VISION AND DREAMS

As Refuge, Reconciliation, Restoration

SLEEP DIDN'T ALWAYS FEEL like refuge. At one point, it became the only place I felt relief. Living with long post-concussion symptoms is a particular kind of exhaustion—the kind that doesn't budge, no matter how much you push through.

Proper sleep isn't just for repairing the body and brain—it restores the body-mind. The mental and emotional layers that quietly shape your habits, reactions, and choices. The forces that move you forward—or keep you suspended. Each night offers a doorway. I didn't understand that until the spring of 2019. I was living in a small room I was renting in Los Angeles, at the base of the Pacific Palisades on the Pacific Coast Highway. Temporary—but I loved it. It became my safe space—despite it technically not being the most safe or secure haven. I was deep in recovery—post-concussion, post-traumatic stress—

and something began to shift during those long, quiet hours.

My days felt stretched. Repetitive. Heavy.

I remember sitting on the floor one afternoon when a friend texted—an invitation to her bachelorette. I couldn't go. From the outside, I looked fine. But I wasn't. Living with an invisible injury is difficult to explain—especially to people you love. There are moments you simply can't show up, no matter how much you want to. I didn't try to explain it. I just said, "You know I'd be there in a heartbeat, but I can't this time." She understood. The people who know you don't need the full story. They just feel it.

To move the energy, I went for long walks at golden hour—one of my favorite things. It wasn't unusual for me to be in bed by 7:30 or 8pm. Not asleep—just winding down, waiting for my body to let go. Observant and aware, I began to see what sleep was doing. I could feel the shift. How it restores a nervous system frayed to the bone. How dreams begin to process what waking life cannot—rewriting, reconciling. How you can wake up—unexpectedly—feeling better. And how that compounds over time. I learned something simple: The mind reveals only what you're ready to face. Until then, something deeper protects you.

After fourteen months of disorientation, something began to reorganize. I started waking differently. Less disoriented. Less exhausted. My lower back—the place where I store emotion—ached less. I could get out of bed without bracing myself first. One morning, sitting with Earl Grey tea and sweet cream, I caught myself laughing mid-sip. Is this really happening? A levitating kind of quiet relief. Night after night, the fog lifted. Clarity returned. My sense of self came back online. Not all at once—but steadily, piece by piece. That's when I understood: Sleep wasn't passive. It was something I could return to—intentionally. A place for reconciliation. Not an escape. An interface.

At the time, I fell asleep listening to Esther Hicks. That rhythm—the repetition—helped. Something about it grounded and comforted me.

Why Dream-state Matters

Dream imagery is potent. It often reflects inner change before waking life does. When the tone of my dreams shifted, so did my inner landscape. There were things I couldn't reconcile in waking life through thinking alone. But in a dream, something moved. Patterns loosened. Things that felt etched into my soul—weren't. Sometimes the shift was immediate. Like a spell breaking—clean and clear. A pattern I had been living inside of simply gone. Not gradual. Not negotiated. Gone. Other times, it unfolded slowly—depending on how deeply something was ingrained, and how willing I was to see it clearly.

While writing this book, I received clarity the same way. One night, three figures surfaced—people I thought I had already released. But something remained. Each one pointed to a place where I was still leaking self-worth. In that state, I saw it clearly—and when I woke up, I acted on it. Done.

What Was Reconciled

- Forgiveness I couldn't reach while awake

- Reconciliation and release
- My self-worth and standards

Layers of the Self

We operate through layers—conscious, subconscious, and beyond. Much of what drives us lives beneath awareness. Patterns. Reactions. Attachments. During one of the lowest points in my recovery, I saw clearly where I was operating from—shame. There was nothing ambiguous about it. I was terrified. Once I saw it, I couldn't stay there.

Dream state became the place where that began to shift. Before I could articulate it. Before I felt safe to be seen. It moved there first—quietly. Later, I could live it out in waking life. Dream state wasn't optional for me. It was essential. Lucid dreaming made it more accessible. I had been doing it since childhood—something that, at the time, worked in my favor.

The Body-mind as a Portal

Healing the mind without tending the body was incomplete. It wasn't either/or. For me, it was both. Memories live in the body—woven through muscle, fascia, bone. Every emotion leaves an imprint. My body was in constant pain. So I worked with it. Stretching. Touch. Body oil. Gua Sha across my muscles. Slowly, I began to feel it shift and release.

In dreams, the body softens its grip. The thinking mind quiets. Something deeper begins to reorganize. The more I cared for my body, the more accessible my inner world became. The more I allowed rest, the more integration happened—without force.

Harmonizing the Mind's Eye

I've always been moved by atmosphere—music, light, place.

There's a song I've loved for years—Dream Machine by Stéphane Pompougnac. I first heard it in Hôtel Costes while staying there in 2011. Something about it stayed with me. That particular night, and point in time—was nothing short of a living dream at a beautiful time in life. Music has a way of pulling you through time. Certain images do the same. Some visions arrive fully formed—and wait.

For a long time, I tried to make sense of everything. When I stopped forcing clarity, it began to arrive on its own. The mind's eye isn't abstract. It sharpens when you stop arguing with what you see. In dreams, this becomes obvious. Symbols appear. Faces return. Scenes rearrange. When I paid attention, patterns revealed themselves—without effort. I stopped trying to manufacture clarity. I allowed it.

Time and Clarity

During recovery, time felt different. Some weeks dragged. Some moments shifted everything overnight. I began to notice something: Clarity changes the pace of things. When a decision was clean, clear and honest—things moved, and rapidly. When I hesitated or was duplicitous, they stalled. Once I realized this, I stopped trying to force outcomes. I chose clarity—and let timing follow.

Your Magnetic Heart

Your heart keeps you alive—but it also tells the truth.

While writing this book, I felt a sharp pain in my chest one afternoon. It stopped me mid-sentence. For a moment, I wondered if my heart would hold. I closed my laptop and wrote a will. I texted the dog's favorite babysitter who is like family with instructions for my little loves should anything happen. Not dramatic. Just clear.

There's something grounding about facing mortality without theatrics. Some parts of life are emotional. Some are administrative. Both matter. That moment brought me back to something simple: The heart signals alignment. During recovery, every sensation was heightened—who and what tightened my chest, and what made me feel calm and safe. And I trusted it.

What Helped

While I could write a book on proper sleep, my preference is to not approach it like a system, but to align with the basics. I adjusted what felt right—and watched what changed.

I stopped eating late.

TV was not even part of the equation.

I became more aware of what I was taking in before sleep—what I thought, what I heard, what I let linger.

Even a few minutes mattered.

I slowed down before bed.

Hot Reishi cocoa. A hot shower. Stillness.

Sometimes I spoke things out loud. Sometimes I didn't.

At times, I recorded my own voice—simple, present-tense thoughts—and fell asleep listening.

Over time, something shifted.
Simply but significantly. And it compounded.

4

CHAPTER FOUR

THE AVATAR

Simply stated—a shift in avatar can be a shift in worlds.
It doesn't need to be a dramatic act.
It's build through habit over time.
While I share an avatar change that created a leap, I have had many avatars before this one that birthed subtle change—that too, eventually had me exit one world and enter another.
It's conscious choice, willingness and commitment—no matter the small step over time or change in the blink of an eye.
The outside catching up with the inside—what was there all along, and re-chosen. Reignited.

THERE's a difference between understanding who you are —and being it. This is about the being. What it looks like moving through the world as yourself. Not conceptually, but actually. I didn't invent this for myself. I started remembering. And it was a choice.

The moment I chose it—fully, deciding to move to the island, and once the decision was made, that was it. Non-negotiable. The timeline was flexible, but I was certain. I didn't know how it would happen—and I didn't need to. I decided, and that was enough. That wasn't my job. My job was to become the version of me who already lived there and had that life.

I started living as her before anything around me had changed. My French neighbor, Mylou, and I would walk our dogs together most days, and sometimes we worked side by side. We spoke about our avatars and vision—who they were, how they lived. Mine surfed more each day. She spoke French. She had a villa of her own—something that felt like my grandparents' farm as a child. A place I didn't want to leave. A place of calm refuge. There was a view. A pool. Space to breathe and walk around barefoot. A place to watch the sunrise and set, and to lay out under the stars. I could feel it clearly. So I began to live in alignment with the avatar. If I was going to surf, I needed to be more flexible. I started doing yoga. I softened—was less rigid, more open. I followed each step as it appeared and prayed constantly—joyfully, in partnership with God.

When it came time to go to the island, I handled what I could—lawyer paperwork, logistics, due diligence. I changed my phone number. Made declarations. Asked for help from various sources—a vulnerable thing. My concierge at the time, Enzo, told me finding a place would be nearly impossible—but showed me where to look. So I did. And then I went one step further. I placed an ad. It was answered. Immediate connection. Immediate yes.

After that, everything required faith—even getting to the airport on that pouring, stormy night when my original transportation failed. None of it was theory. It was faith. I kept being her, even when it felt premature. Even when nothing was fully secured.

There's a tipping point—where the old identity no longer holds, and the new one hasn't fully landed yet. That space is uncomfortable. I remember sitting in it—knowing I couldn't go back, and not yet knowing how I would move forward. For me, it felt like dying. Letting go of a life I had tried to make work—a life that wasn't bad, but underneath it, I was exhausted. Bruised. Not alive at all. I couldn't carry it forward any longer.

Leaving was not an escape. It was survival. I had help at every step—because I asked, and did the work, my part. People who showed up at the exact moment I needed them. They know who they are. And I'll never forget it.

The body is always communicating. During that time, I started to notice it more clearly—what felt aligned, and what didn't. What expanded me, and what contracted me. That which was aligned happened easily and rapidly. If support was needed, it appeared. The which was meant to crumble and fold—did, on its own. That which is meant to be buried will dig its own grave if you let it.

When the signal is clear, you don't need to overthink. You feel it. Stay—or move. Ease—or friction. That clarity became my guide. In 2019 one of the phrases that dropped into my psyche was, "clarity, peace and results". It's all I wanted in a sea of prolonged head injury symptoms. Staying committed to that—what I prayed for, even when I wasn't clear about the specifics, it all caught up years later.

I didn't build this identity from scratch. I uncovered it. It revealed itself through what I wanted—and through what I could no longer tolerate. Who was I before I adapted? Before I adjusted to fit? That question changes things.

You are living a story. The themes repeat until they are understood. The characters return until something shifts. At some point you ask: was I cast in this role—or did I consent to it? That question alone changes the plot.

My avatar existed long before I consciously met it. As a child, I was one with it. Somewhere along the way, I lost it. Then—during recovery—it returned. Not quietly. Viscerally. Stable on the inside. Wobbly on the outside. Relearning my legs and my voice. Energy was minimal. Thoughts arriving faster than speech could carry them. I often felt like a mental patient in an open-air prison—yet at the same time, deeply aware of how alive I was. That paradox reshaped me. The avatar didn't arrive as invention. It returned as recognition—sensation, snapshots, memory.

In 2018 after my accident, my sense of self fractured—and then slowly came back together. I could see the layers: mental, emotional, physical, energetic. When they were aligned, I felt steady. When they weren't, everything felt off. So I began asking simple questions: What feels better? What brings more peace? Not as theory—but as practice.

Integration doesn't live in isolation. It shows up in how you walk into a room. How you speak. How you choose. How you move through ordinary moments defines your life. Not the big ones—the small ones. When identity is unclear, everything feels off. When it's steady, there's nothing to prove. Who you are behind closed doors—and who you are in front of others—begins to match. And when it does, everything requires less effort. Things just move.

This isn't about performance. It's about consistency and truth. Identity isn't what you declare once—it's what you live repeatedly.

One of my favorite daily practices is simple:

"God, have me be an angel in someone's life today."

Small actions become miracles in other people's worlds. My mother taught me this. She lived half her life with a kidney condition and never complained. She played full out—never a victim of circumstance. Her way of being instilled in me perseverance, rigor, and an intolerance for unnecessary suffering when solutions exist. Live in a way that honors those who didn't get more time.

Identity without embodiment is just a dream. You put on your personality each day the way you choose clothing. You decide the energy, the tone, the posture. The level of care. You breathe life into it.

If your daily life isn't aligned with who you claim to be, what are you selling out for? Mind the ego—it's clever. It disguises itself as normal, as conformity, as safety. When you look in the mirror, do your eyes light up—or do they go flat?

In Motion

Sometimes embodiment reveals itself most clearly when it's put to the test—not in ceremony, not in safe places, but out in the wild, where you can't shrink. It was a party.

Fall 2019. I was invited by a friend of the host—someone I knew well. I'm an introverted homebody who's often told I live my life like an adventure. I also love a good social gathering. This night stood out. It was one of my first ventures back into the world after my head injury—living with limited executive functioning and sustained post-traumatic stress.

A portion of a restaurant had been rented for a birthday. I wore what I would normally wear to dinner there on a Thursday night. Simple. Understated. Effortless—slightly undone rocker chic but intentionally put together, the way I normally show up. Before leaving, I looked in the mirror and thought, Gosh, I look tired.

And then: I'm so grateful to be going out. I'm still me. For a second, I almost didn't go. Tired meant living with constant traumatic stress moving through my body. Unrested. Malnourished. In survival mode. Still—me. When I checked my coat and walked into the room, I realized instantly that I was underdressed. No dress code had been shared. Everyone else was in full cocktail attire—head-to-toe luxury. I had a choice. I could shrink—or I could own who I was.

There was a split-second wobble of insecurity—and then I snapped back into my body. I felt it in my chest—tight, familiar. I softened my shoulders and stood straighter. I may not be dressed to code, I thought—but no one here can be me. Even at my lowest, I wouldn't have traded lives with anyone in the room. That night had nothing to do with clothing. It had everything to do with embodiment—anchoring into something real when unease knocked.

Owning who you are—in real time—is magnetic. No one can take that from you. Self-love isn't something that arrives—it's something you choose. Who do you see when you look in the mirror? Do you meet your own eyes—or look away? It took me years to say I unconditionally loved the person looking back at me. Now, I do. Transformation doesn't require mourning. It requires honesty. You don't need to leave parts of yourself behind to evolve. You can carry them forward with you.

Who you are is a creative process. Every quality you admire in others is a clue—not a comparison. We all have shadows. The work isn't eliminating them—it's integrating them. Shadow is where unclaimed power lives. Integration makes you whole. Desire is not passive. It is directive. At a certain point, the work is no longer about becoming. It's about living as.

I felt it before I could explain it.

I didn't become someone new.

I became someone I already was.

PART IV: ASCEND

RIDE THE WAVES

1
RIGHT ON TIME

Once you see clearly—you don't go back.
You don't move the same way anymore.
This is where everything you've seen, felt, and understood
—becomes real. You start living.

In the Game

NOTHING BREAKS the soul like hesitation—waking up years later wishing you had simply gone for it, wondering if it's too late now. It doesn't matter when this realization happens. What matters is that it does.

I was six when I first learned this.

I had been taking dance lessons, and the following year I refused to go back because I heard my teacher wasn't returning. No one else would do. I cried a full-body cry in my mom's arms. It wouldn't be the same without Miss Nicole. She did come back. I never got the memo. At the end of the year, I sat in the audience watching the recital I was supposed to be in. I burned with regret. That was the day I decided: I will not sit on the sidelines of my own life. And I haven't since. The truth stabilizes you.

There's Always a Price

Since 2018, I have lived inside extended uncertainty—until very recently. There was no alternative. Certainty had to be built internally. A quiet, unwavering knowing—without proof, without timeline, without guarantees. Safety within—not external.

The price of not moving forward would have cost me my life—the way it was already costing me. A slow bleed. The light on, but no one home.

When you step out of body and look back at yourself clearly, the choice becomes simple. You either trade comfort for truth—or you trade your life for illusion.

Into Form

I used to think "happily ever after" was a picture.

It isn't. It's a feeling. And when you feel it—even briefly—you recognize it immediately.

Refine the self and be ready.

This morning, I woke from a lucid dream—curious, calm. A Christmas morning-like feeling. It was one of those dreams where something fused for certain: what the subconscious has been holding and what consciousness has finally allowed. Something important that I planted took root. This was an exciting—and honestly relieving—moment. Something I've wanted—forever, but hadn't been ready to hold—arrived. In that moment I realized: I've done the work. When it arrives, I'll be able to hold it. The image now lives inside me—impressed like a memory of the future.

Sometimes the most vivid visions are simple. They come when you least expect them. Receiving an image instead of forcing a thought changes everything. Remember who you are—and stop sabotaging yourself to protect your heart—or any other part of your life. The fear is false.

You don't need more time.
You don't need more proof.
You already know what to do.
What you've been waiting for—
is allowing yourself to say yes.
Stop delaying what's already clear.
Stop choosing what is comfortable over what is true.
Remember who you are—
and watch the world rearrange to meet you.

Enough

Ms. Whitney Houston has appeared at multiple pivotal moments in my life—like an electrical surge moving through my body, safely guiding me.

I remember being six years old, standing on stage under bright lights in my sequins, dancing to I Wanna Dance With Somebody. It was our dance studio's year-end grand finale. I never wanted that moment—or that season—to end.

Years later, in 2017, her voice found me again during a time that cracked me open and became the foundation of who I am.

And then again in 2023—on a flight home from St. Barths. Suspended somewhere between where I had been and where I was going, six months before I would move there and change my life.

Perfect timing. Every time. God speaking through her.

At her funeral, Kevin Costner shared a private moment from her audition for The Bodyguard.

Even Whitney—her voice, her iconic, effortlessly show-stopping presence—was quietly asking:

Am I good enough?

Am I pretty enough?

Will they like me?

A thousand small doubts. The kind so many of us carry.

And the answer—spoken to her, but meant for all of us:

You weren't just good enough.

You were great.

Perfection is achieved, not when there is nothing more to add, but when there is nothing left to take away.

—Antoine de Saint-Exupéry

www.ingramcontent.com/pod-product-compliance
Lightning Source LLC
LaVergne TN
LVHW090607110826
845146LV00001B/289

* 9 7 9 8 9 9 3 3 3 1 0 0 3 *